TEACHING WHAT THEY LEARN, LEARNING WHAT THEY LIVE

HOW TEACHERS' PERSONAL HISTORIES SHAPE THEIR PROFESSIONAL DEVELOPMENT

BRAD OLSEN

Paradigm Publishers

Boulder • London

Copyright © 2008 Paradigm Publishers

Published in the United States by Paradigm Publishers, 3360 Mitchell Lane, Suite E, Boulder, CO 80301 USA.

Paradigm Publishers is the trade name of Birkenkamp & Company, LLC, Dean Birkenkamp, President and Publisher.

Library of Congress Cataloging-in-Publication Data
Olsen, Brad.
  Teaching what they learn, learning what they live : how teachers' personal histories shape their professional development / Brad Olsen.
    p. cm.
  Includes bibliographical references and index.
  ISBN 978-1-59451-536-1 (hardcover)
  1. First year teachers—United States. 2. Teaching. I. Title.
  LB2844.1.N4O45 2008
  371.1—dc22

                                                        2007046102

Printed and bound in the United States of America on acid-free paper that meets the standards of the American National Standard for Permanence of Paper for Printed Library Materials.

Designed and typeset by Straight Creek Bookmakers.

12 11 10 09 08   1 2 3 4 5

Contents

Foreword

This book reads like a fast-paced novel, revealing layers of complexity—about four beginning teachers, their prior learning, and the interaction of their teacher education programs on their growing knowledge. *Teaching What They Learn, Learning What They Live* provoked a strong feeling of identification in me, as it reminded me of the passion and concern that I had more than twenty years ago when Lynne Miller and I wrote our little book entitled *Teachers: Their World and Their Work.*

It was 1984, and we were trying to capture the knowledge of teachers, arguing that without it, it would be difficult to improve schools. Our concern then was that there was little or no recognition of the real life of the teacher within the culture of schools. We had both been teachers in elementary and secondary schools, and nothing in the public debate described our lives as we lived them in our respective schools. But the context was different. *A Nation at Risk* had just been published, describing a "crisis" in the schools. The effects of this document were to mandate more courses, more tests, more standards, more requirements, and more control over schools and teachers. Schools were blamed for the decline of the nation, and by implication, the teachers were at fault. At the same time, the Carnegie Task Force issued *A Nation Prepared.* This monograph focused on the social world of the schools, particularly the way the role of the teacher had come to be defined. They argued for a new professionalism, for the creation of new leadership roles within the teaching ranks, and for the development of teacher-initiated reforms.

Within this context we wrote that it was important to describe the lived world of the teacher in both elementary and secondary schools. Understanding what teaching was really like, in all its complexity, was missing from the conversation about educational change and improvement. Both these views were strong and vocal—to do more of the same and to focus more deeply on the role and knowledge of the teacher.

Now, more than twenty years later, the same themes are evident, but they have taken on a different look. *No Child Left Behind* (NCLB) is the law of the land pressing for the education of all children, no matter what their background or circumstance. The means for doing this are to hold schools accountable with a massive testing program and a focus on reading and math. Along with these foci, there is also a turn toward blaming teacher education programs for the failure to provide *quality teachers* who can educate all children and a consequent acceptance of the old shibboleth that *anyone can teach*. At the same time, there is a strong press to create professional learning communities, grow reflective practitioners, and create a culture among teachers to share leadership in improving schools for all students. Within this context, there is a need for less blame and greater understanding of how teachers learn, for understanding what supports they need, and for discovering how to get at the nuances of programs that engage both the personal and professional issues that are a part of becoming a teacher.

Brad Olsen's intelligent book does just this as he takes on the growth and development of beginning teachers, focusing on a broader view of what counts as teacher knowledge. He asks the big questions up front. What is knowledge? How does a beginning teacher's knowledge emerge? What are teachers' incoming conceptions about teaching, learning, subject matter, and schooling? How do their teacher education programs interact with their incoming dispositions and influences? And he sets about to answer these critical questions through an in-depth study of one secondary teacher and three others engaged in different teacher education programs. His analysis is grounded in two years of investigation, providing us with a cogent, interesting, and provocative explanation of the significant questions that he poses.

We follow with great anticipation as Liz becomes a teacher in her first secondary English class. We feel her struggle to somehow deal with the conflicting influences of her own biography and her teacher education program. We learn how powerfully her own dispositions trump her teacher education program. We watch her deal with the social realities of a classroom of students whose backgrounds differ from hers. In one sense Liz is unique, but in another, she is typical of all those who become teachers. She must deal with her own dispositions and the influences of her biography and figure out how to incorporate her new learning into a teaching style. Teacher education programs can help beginning teachers by engaging them in understanding the tensions that arise from their knowledge (or lack of it) of students, subject matter, schooling, and their own life histories. They, too, must understand the limitations as well as the possibilities these influences offer to the beginning teacher. These important insights make visible how beginning teachers gain knowledge and what roles teacher education programs play. Everyone is up for scrutiny and deeper understanding—teacher candidates and teacher education programs!

This view of the growth of teacher knowledge, as Olsen reminds us, is "wider, deeper, holistic, and spiraling." It is this kind of understanding of what it means to learn to teach that we need to help provide access to. His book enriches us all about the work that needs to be accomplished to improve teaching, teacher education, and, ultimately, our schools.

—*Ann Lieberman,*
senior scholar at the Carnegie Foundation
for the Advancement of Teaching

Acknowledgments

This book began as a doctoral dissertation at the University of California, Berkeley, and neither the dissertation nor this book would have been possible without the bighearted support, guidance, and assistance provided by many. I will forever be in debt to the following people, who helped me to research, teach, write, remain sane, and enjoy my work (and to realize that such distinctions cannot easily be drawn): Jeanine, my family, and friends. Professors Judith Warren Little, Sarah Warshauer Freedman, Dan Perlstein, Paul Ammon, and Jeannie Oakes. The teachers in this project, who shared their time and perspectives with me. Dena Sexton for her proofreading help. And Beth Davis for her useful editorial assistance.

Introduction
Teachers, Teaching, and Teacher Education

Educational change depends on what teachers think and do—
it's as simple and as complex as that.

— *Michael Fullan (1991)*

Teacher preparation is perhaps now more crucial than ever. The number of new teachers hired in U.S. public schools these days is staggering. For the 1990–1999 decade, more than 2 million new teachers were hired (Gerald and Hussar 1998); for the present decade an expected 1.6 million new teachers will be added (Hussar and Bailey 2006). The numbers in 1990–1999 represented a 35 percent rise over the number of new teachers hired between 1980 and 1989 (Husser and Bailey 2006; Murname et al. 1991). Jeannie Oakes and Martin Lipton (2003) observed that the new teachers prepared at this recent turn of the century will, by 2007, "comprise about half of all public school teachers in the nation" (xvii). This is mostly because current teachers of the baby boom era are approaching retirement age, and because student enrollments are steadily rising (Gerald and Hussar 1998). There are other factors, too, though their impact is not as great. They include the fact that more special education and special pullout programs that require teachers are being established (Gerald and Hussar 1998), as well as the fact that many states have been implementing class-size reduction policies, which, as they reduce the number of students in a classroom, increase the number of teachers required (Blattner, Hall, and Reinhard 1997; Wexler et al. 1998).

Furthermore, teacher attrition has become a significant concern. It has been reported that 30 percent of new teachers leave the profession before their third year and 46 percent leave before their fifth year (Ingersoll 2003, 2004). So ubiquitous, teacher attrition is now often referred to by its shorthand metaphor—the "revolving door" of teaching. And teacher turnover is especially significant in high-poverty, urban schools. Of all public schools, those located in urban, low-income communities face the highest turnover rates and staffing problems (Carroll et al. 2000; Hanushek, Kain, and Rivkin 2001; Henke, Chen, and Geis 2000; Lankford, Loeb, and Wykoff 2002; NCTAF 2003). On the whole, teachers in high-poverty urban schools are as much as 50 percent more likely to leave than those in lower-poverty schools (Ingersoll 2003, 2004). In response to losing disproportionate numbers of teachers each year, high-poverty urban schools often fill resulting vacancies with underqualified teachers, who not only are less prepared to teach, but also leave schools at significantly higher rates than their certified peers (Darling-Hammond 2000).

It is for these reasons that teacher education has lately become the focus of significant attention and debate.

* * *

Teacher education in the United States formally began in the middle of the nineteenth century. Teacher preparation was initially considered the province of so-called normal schools—private or public vocational institutions charged with supplying the country with its (mostly female) teachers. By 1940, however, most normal schools had been replaced by and/or renamed teachers colleges, and most of these teachers colleges, themselves, were soon absorbed into universities (Clifford and Guthrie 1988; Herbst 1991). These teacher training sites moved onto university campuses, because each entity believed it had something to gain from the incorporation. The teachers colleges stood to benefit from the academic status and resources of universities, and the higher education campuses could include the mostly female teaching students in their gender-equity accounting and also stood to benefit from the added tuition these students would bring. In their book *Ed School*, Geraldine Clifford and James Guthrie (1988) discuss the ensuing decades of teacher education and education schools as structured by inverse relationships between status and practicality, cognate disciplines and professional schools, stasis and change.

Teacher education programs have come in all shapes and sizes over the last eighty years, but have consisted mainly of differing equations of four primary approaches to teacher learning. Sharon Feiman-Nemser (1990) names those approaches the *academic orientation* (transmitting professional knowledge to the teacher), the *personal orientation* (focusing on the teacher's own development), the *critical orientation* (coupling social change with a radical critique of schooling), and the *technological orientation* (identifying what the science of teaching has uncovered). Kenneth Zeichner (1992) identified four similar strands: the academic tradition, developmental tradition, social reconstructionist tradition, and social efficiency tradition. No matter the terminology, these four enduring models of teacher education have combined in various, sometimes competing ways over the years. Most teacher education programs participate, to some degree, in all four thematic strands, but each program tips its balance in favor of one or two at the expense of the others (for more about teacher education approaches, see Cochran-Smith and Zeichner 2005).

And, finally, teacher education has recently been under the political gun, as the influence of education unions has diminished and political conservatives have called for complete overhauls, or the wholesale elimination, of university teacher education (e.g., Ballou and Podursky 2000; Hess 2001). Consider former U.S. education secretary Rod Paige infamously calling the National Education Association a "terrorist organization" while addressing a group of governors (King 2004). Or note conservative columnist George Will (2006) claiming that "the surest, quickest way to add quality to primary and secondary education would be addition by subtraction: Close all the schools of education." Over the last decade, especially, many states have decreased both the autonomy and authority of university teacher education programs by changing teacher licensing requirements, standardizing teacher education procedures, and deprofessionalizing careers in teaching (U.S. Department of Education 2002). Additionally (and not unconnectedly), alternative or so-called backdoor entries into teaching, like *Teach for America* or district internship programs; debates about the overall effectiveness of teachers; and heated critiques of education from both the political left and right continue to garner big headlines and produce highly charged discussion on all sides. One example is the *No Child Left Behind Act*, which has become a lightning rod for politicized attempts to define and measure "highly qualified teachers" and reprofessionalize teaching by expanding student testing and scripted teaching programs (U.S. Department of Education n.d.)

All these competing perspectives and political agendas, plus the fierce passions on all sides, can make for an extremely complex and highly charged landscape of preparing today's teachers for their professional work in public classrooms. It is into this fray that I wish to place this book. It seems to me that empirical study around these questions must work to ferret out and identify the political demands, the sociocultural foundations, and the competing truths that become interwoven in most of these debates. Systematic investigation of teacher preparation is paramount, and empirical studies of the processes and effects of teacher education should be central. This book is an attempt to supplement existing discussions by providing a descriptive, analytical treatment of learning to teach—one whose findings offer a richer portrait of professional preparation and ways in which teacher education does matter, but not always, and not necessarily in the ways intended. The goal of this book is to deepen and broaden the conversation about exactly how novices committed to teaching become beginning teachers. By presenting an empirical, ecological exploration of learning-to-teach, this book hopes to deepen understanding of the professional learning of beginning teachers.

* * *

Teaching is difficult, and teacher education is difficult. Teaching is an enormously complex activity. It requires use of intellect, emotions, intuition, the senses, previous experience, judgment, knowledge of content and context and kids, kinesthetics, creativity, personality, and linguistic performance. Typically, several of these abilities combine; many times all thirteen are called into simultaneous use. Teachers work with dozens of children at a time, and the children typically vary in ability, maturity, background, and personality—and many do not want to be in school. Moreover, teaching occurs within multiple, often competing, organizational and political contexts, exerting both direct and mediating forces on what teachers think and do. These complexities not only problematize the act of teaching, they also make the study of teaching a challenge.

Several generations of research on teaching, including process-product research, time on task, and cognition-and-mediation paradigms (Lagemann 2000; Shulman 1986b; Zeichner 1999), have been unable to fully capture what teachers do. Both quantitative and qualitative approaches include sacrifices and methodological limitations (Bogdan and Biklen 1998). Researcher bias can never be entirely eliminated (Becker 1998; Erickson 1986; Geertz 1973). The currently fashionable ethnographic approach, although making strides in casting its research net broadly to embrace the holistic, cultural web in which teachers think and act, still struggles to find conceptual models both wide enough to include all variables and deep enough to have sufficient explanatory power (Wideen,

Mayer-Smith, and Moon 1998). And so the complexity makes teaching nearly impossible to wholly deconstruct, analyze, or fully articulate—additionally handicapping attempts to measure, reward, or even talk about the practice of teaching to others. Its complexity is part of the reason (along with a host of sociohistorical, economic, and political factors) why preparing successful teachers has been a perennial struggle.

To teach teaching, one must first be able to identify what teaching is in ways that are analyzable, articulatable, and transferable to others. Its complexity hinders, if not fully sabotages, these activities. To be concerned with teaching is to inevitably confront the domain of teacher preparation: How does professional learning relate to practice? In what ways (if at all) do teachers' formal education experiences influence their subsequent teaching? What is learning-to-teach, really?

Most educators and education researchers acknowledge that preservice teacher education is neither simple nor effortless. The apprenticeship of observation, or teachers teaching how they were taught—first chronicled by Dan Lortie (1975)—has been widely discussed in the quarter century since (Cuban 1993; Fuller and Bown 1975; Sarason 1981). The resiliency of prospective teachers' prior beliefs has been extensively examined over the last few decades (Bird et al. 1993; Britzman 1986; Holt-Reynolds 1992; Pajares 1992; Weinstein 1989). The weakness of teacher education as an interruption is often asserted (Rust 1994; Zeichner and Gore 1990; Zeichner and Tabachnick 1981). These are potent findings with far-reaching implications for teacher education attitudes and policies, and they deserve continuous examination. With the study on which this book reports I sought to examine what occurs as a handful of novices over time become beginning professionals. What does teacher development look like in practice? In what ways do beginning teachers rely on prior understandings as they construct their professional knowledge? What is teacher knowledge? What do we really mean when we talk about beginning teacher learning?

This book reports on an investigation of how, and from where, a beginning teacher's knowledge emerges. The book reports on a four-year research project in which eight beginning English teachers at four different university teacher preparation programs in California were studied over two years in order to investigate their professional development. The study was an exploration of the multiple social, epistemological, and cognitive domains that comprise learning-to-teach. Primary focus was placed on examining ways in which beginning teachers' *personal* dispositions and conceptions (deriving from their life histories and sociocultural contexts) combined with their teacher preparation programs' *professional* approaches and contexts to form each beginning teacher's knowledge of and orientations toward teaching, learning, subject, students, and multiculturalism.

With this book I hope to recast learning-to-teach as a continuous, situated, holistic knowledge-and-identity process, in which prior experiences produce deeply embedded ways of viewing the world that go on to organize current/future experience into meaning. One's past shapes how one learns and, therefore, directs the contours of one's particular teacher preparation experience. Following this, I share analyses and stories of the learning conflicts, patterns, and events that constituted the teacher preparation experiences for four beginning high school English teachers in urban northern California. Recounting and analyzing these teachers' experiences, the book demonstrates that learning-to-teach is not a direct, cognitive process of internalizing knowledge but a circular, holistic process of negotiating among often competing knowledge sources and contexts. Traditional notions of professional learning cannot account for these teachers' preparation experiences. Indeed, this study demonstrates that professional learning is less about accruing technical or intellectual knowledge and more about (re-)constructing one's own teacher identity. In fact, following the findings of this study, I use this book to demonstrate that "identity" is a more useful analytic than "knowledge," and that "teacher identity development"—or its synonym, "teachers' professional identity development"—is more useful than the antiquated "teacher learning."

This book is organized to simultaneously present the study, analyze multiple facets of teacher development, and illuminate ways in which beginning teachers construct their professional identities out of myriad influences and processes. *Chapter one* discusses several traditions of philosophy, cognition, and social theory, which inform the theoretical framing of teacher learning/identity adopted in the study. *Chapter two* tells the two-year story of one teacher in the study in order to empirically illustrate the situated, iterative process of knowledge development presented in chapter one. *Chapter three* presents a cross-case analysis of four of the teachers—each from a different teacher education program—to examine how personal history and teacher preparation program interrelate to form a teacher's professional identity. *Chapter four* amplifies principal themes from the study and offers three corresponding discussions for practice: (1) how teachers can increase their understandings of—and control over—ways their personal histories shape their professional development, (2) how teacher educators might better align teacher education with actual ways beginners construct teacher knowledge, and (3) how researchers might consider "teacher identity" a more useful conception than teacher knowledge. And, finally, the appendix offers a methodological discussion of the research procedures and presumptions I employed.

I arrive at the study of teacher preparation as both a qualitative researcher and a teacher educator, someone drawn with equal pull toward opportunities to systematically investigate teacher learning and, just as important, implement what I find. That these interests are complementary fortuitously positions me within a currently popular landscape of inquiry that attempts to link research and practice and has become increasingly bent on challenging boundaries—between theory and practice, between the professional and the personal, between the past and the present. It is my hope that this book can participate in the ever-evolving conversations around teaching, learning, teacher education, and conducting research on teacher development.

1

Theories of Knowing, Learning, and Teacher Knowledge

We don't see things as they are, we see them as we are.

—*Anaïs Nin*

This new millennium finds teacher learning researchers and teacher educators inside several related theoretical revolutions. Within cognition and epistemology, vestiges of the earlier knowledge transfer model are being replaced by constructivist and poststructuralist views, suggesting that learning is a process of creating knowledge rather than acquiring it and is a social process as much as an individual one. Within teacher education and professional development, political debates about who "owns" teacher knowledge have combined with empirical debates about how teachers think and learn, resulting in the ascendance of the teacher as a significant knowledge producer and knowledge-in-use (or "local" knowledge) as a leading unit of analysis. In many teacher education and school restructuring policy arenas, teachers are now considered less as passive, interchangeable automatons in education and more as active, unique persons with great influence over how student learning unfolds. And, finally, the emerging visibility of embedded, reciprocal relationships among all aspects of life has eroded boundaries between the personal and professional, between private and public, self and other, and has therefore called for a research paradigm holistic enough to consider the teacher as whole person, over time, in context. I view this present convergence of research traditions as creating a landscape fertile for ecological investigations of how teachers develop and use their professional knowledge. As well, this convergence requires that we consider knowledge, and teacher knowledge, differently than has typically been the case.

In this first chapter, I trace the theoretical traditions of inquiry, which, taken together, lead to a conclusion that teacher knowledge is holistic, situated, and continuous. It is my belief that epistemology, cognition, and social theory have currently arrived at a place where one might conceive of knowledge as deriving from multiple aspects of a teacher's identity, embedded in practice, and iteratively structured. Yet, those three related evolutions have not been direct, nor have they reached their termination. The discussion is organized to illustrate currently held notions of teacher epistemology and cognition in the United States as having a Western history structured by dual tensions between empiricism and rationalism—in other words, between situatedness and abstraction—yet simultaneously influenced by Eastern notions of holism and harmony, as well. I then continue by presenting my own empirically derived formulations of teacher knowledge, teacher learning, and the role of prior knowledge in teacher development. In presenting these formulations I hope to offer some philosophical and historical grounding that will enrich understandings of how teachers think and learn in situ. My goal is both to present the theoretical foundation upon which the subsequent chapters sit and to convince educators to adopt a view of teacher knowledge that is broader, deeper, more holistic, and more spiraling than the often linear, abstract, discrete views of knowledge typically enacted (consciously or not) in teacher education and the research on learning-to-teach.

Related Traditions of Inquiry Inform
Research on Teacher Knowledge

In the 1970s, as backlash against what they believed an overly behavioristic approach to the study of teaching, several education theorists initiated research and discussion on *teacher thinking*, therefore introducing cognition to the modern research movement on teaching, as well as foregrounding knowledge as a legitimate object of analysis (Clark and Yinger 1979; Good, Biddle, and Brophy 1978; Shavelson and Stern 1981). These researchers began asking the questions "How does teacher thinking relate to student achievement?" and "What does an effective teacher know?" *Teacher knowledge* researchers picked this up in the 1980s and started asking, "What is teacher knowledge?" "Where does it come from?" and

"What does a teacher need to know?" (Clandinin 1985; Feiman-Nemser and Buchmann 1985; Grossman 1990; Shulman 1986a, 1987; Wilson, Shulman, and Richert 1987). Simultaneously, since Kurt Lewin (1948), action research—or *teacher research* (Cochran-Smith and Lytle 1993; Stenhouse 1975) has been challenging existing views about where and how, and by whom, teaching knowledge is created, often arguing that teacher knowledge derives from teachers practicing in classrooms as much as (or more than) from professors writing in universities.[1]

Underneath these modern lines of inquiry sit a century of research on cognition and about 2,500 years of epistemology, which together explore the fundamental question "What is knowledge?" Thinkers from Plato and Aristotle, through Kant and Locke, to Dewey and Lave and Wenger have examined whether knowledge is empirical or rational, created or acquired, forged in the mind or blended together in social settings—or whether such a thing as knowledge even exists. Ways of conceiving teacher knowledge have been refined to a point where entire debates turn on whether, in obtaining knowledge, one "constructs" it, "produces" it, "acquires" it, or "internalizes" it. During 1998–2000, for example, *Educational Researcher* published five articles weighing in on whether, to describe learning, the accurate adjective is "*situated*" or "*cognitive*" (Anderson et al. 2000; Cobb and Bowers 1999; Kirshner and Whitson 1998; Korthagan and Kessels 1999; Putnam and Borko 2000). I do not mean to imply that games of semantics have replaced substantive debates on knowledge; in fact, I intend the opposite: Our understanding of the topic has evolved to a sophisticated level where we can now distinguish among subtle, yet fundamental, characteristics of the knowledge process.

And, finally, contributions from critical theory have introduced consideration of how language, power, and cultural positioning reciprocally influence ways in which humans reflect on and enact knowledge, thinking, and learning (Bourdieu 1991; Fairclough 1989; Foucault 1970, 1977; Lyotard 1984/1979; Popkewitz and Brennan 1998). This loosely connected cluster of theories highlights active roles that status; social relations; economics; language; history; and the resulting fragile, asymmetrical balances of power play in any aspect of social existence—even going so far as to reject the very notion of an individual (Foucault arguing that nothing exists outside of the always social discourse [1970], or Bakhtin's belief that all we say has been previously authored [in Holquist 1990]). Applied to teacher knowledge, this critical theory perspective not only informs critical pedagogues and action research advocates who use power relations to help explain whose teacher knowledge becomes valued, but also beckons education researchers to more thoroughly and ecologically examine how an individual both influences and is influenced by others and by past and present sociocultural contexts (Apple 1999; Cochran-Smith and Lytle 1993, 1999).

Epistemological Theories of Knowledge

Epistemology came into being in 350 BC with Plato's *Meno* (Gardner 1985). Plato viewed knowledge—or "wisdom," from the Greek *sophia*—as knowledge of the whole, whereas Aristotle viewed wisdom instead as knowledge of causes. Plato believed we cannot have true knowledge of anything that is in a constant state of change—for example, the world of our senses—and so he conceived of knowledge as an *understanding of the ideas out of which* things are created: the deeper "stuff" of which all things are a part. This understanding later came to be called "reason." As Jostein Gaardner (1996) wrote: "[For Plato], first came the idea of 'horse,' then came all the sensory world's horses trotting along like shadows on a cave wall." Plato therefore viewed knowledge as reason-based.

Aristotle, however, believed Plato had it backward. Aristotle agreed with the distinction between a tangible thing (the horse, if we pick up Gaardner's example) and its essence (the idea of "horse"), but believed that the idea, or essence, of the thing *followed from* having first perceived several tangible examples of the thing. That is, the idea "horse" is simply an aggregated concept arising out of our actually having seen a number of horses. For Aristotle, then, knowledge was the grasping of the idea of the thing out of enough examples of the thing itself. In his view, sensory experience *precedes* any grasp of the concept. Aristotle viewed knowledge as experience-based. Aristotle was an early empiricist, whereas Plato was an early rationalist.

This fundamental distinction between knowledge as deriving from an internal logic, or reason (Plato's rationalism), and knowledge as deriving from external sensory perceptions, or experience (Aristotle's empiricism), has structured epistemological debates ever since. It is a binary worth keeping in mind, as it proves useful when exploring the research on teacher development, because it assists us in distinguishing between competing theories of education. For example, many conceptions of the learning-to-teach process that rely primarily on learning from classroom or personal experience can be seen as deriving from empiricist notions of knowledge. John Dewey's (1933) instrumentalism is one such model. Paulo Freire's (1970) authority of experience is another. Both can be described as Aristotelian in their epistemology, whereas, on the other side, "banking" (Freire 1970) and "mind-as-storehouse" (Cuban 1993) conceptions of teaching, or George Counts's social meliorist movement (Kliebard 1995), are more Platonic.

Descartes's Mind/Body Dualism

Arguably, much of the last 350 years of philosophy and the whole history of social psychology have been an attempt to undo Descartes (Popkewitz 2001). René Descartes's (1637) famous binary separating mind and body established at least the perception of a split between knowledge and experience, between internal thought and external world. Accepting this split means accepting that mind (and therefore thinking, meaning, and knowledge) exists separately from the body (a corporeal realm that includes sensation, experience, and the external world). Descartes argued that *body* is an extended entity existing in reference to space and time, whereas *mind* is an ethereal, unextended "thinking thing" that requires neither space nor time to exist (Descartes 1637). Epistemology has forever since been trying to rejoin the two phenomena and convince us that no binary exists—that existing in the world and making meaning are united.

Immanuel Kant (2003/1781) disputed Descartes by arguing that knowledge must be understood as a product of both understanding (or logic) and experience (or sensation). He posited the parallel existence of two realities: a noumenal one, existing independent of human sensation, and the phenomenal one we perceive through our senses. Yet, the only one we can know is that latter one—one *we ourselves construct* from the relationship between thought and sense, from the empirical phenomena we perceive and the rationalist meaning we attach to them. Kant synthesized Plato's rationalism and Aristotle's empiricism. Put another way, and what Kant himself termed the Kantian Revolution (after Copernicus's famous paradigm shift), human understanding does not *derive from* the material world; the material world is *created out of* human understanding. "Kant placed knowledge in the mind of the active thinker," wrote Howard Gardner (1985, 59). In making this point, Kant collapsed the binary between thought and experience and introduced the notion that thought creates experience as much as experience creates thought. The two occurrences, he believed, are inseparable.

Martin Heidegger (1997/1927) also rejected the Cartesian mind/body dualism, believing that humans do not live apart from existence—observing and interacting with it—but rather humans *are* their existence, creating the worlds they inhabit out of their interpretations of events. Heidegger held that as we go through life, we are continually evaluating and reevaluating, assembling and reassembling our selves in an attempt to carve out an authentic existence in relation to things-that-are (i.e., the real situations we encounter). Epistemology becomes ontology. Interpretation constitutes reality. The present always links to the past, because each of us remains in part bound by our previous assemblages of a self while we reconstruct our selves within any present experience. The present, Heidegger argued, involves a dynamic interplay of past, present, and future. It is related to a past-made-present and a future-already-possessed in the prediction of events and consequences encountered.

A similarly constructivist explanation of knowledge and being comes from psychologist George Kelly (1955, 1963). Kelly begins with the elegant (but gendered) premise that "each man contemplates in his own personal way the stream of events upon which he finds himself so swiftly borne." He proceeds to argue that an individual approaches any experience already in possession of a transparent organizing pattern or template (he uses "*construct*") of the world that is used to perceive, interpret, and make meaning of experience. Because humans are inherently scientists (unconsciously possessing desires to "predict and control," he wrote), an owner continually—and automatically—tests his or her construct for its accuracy to predict events and interpretations and seeks to revise the construct if needed. However, because we cannot help but evaluate our constructs *using our own constructs,* they become self-reinforcing—always concluding that what we perceive the way we perceive it is, in fact, what exists.[2] Such, he argued, is how we move through the world. He argued that each of us creates our particular way of interpreting events of the world unconsciously from early lived experiences. These interpretive patterns he called "life themes." He argued that, because one's life themes produce specific ways of interpreting experience, biography and knowing are inextricably linked.

Descartes was wrong, but his dualism was a crucial step in the evolution of epistemology. It allowed others to come along and—by refining, refuting, or replacing his ideas—move the philosophy of knowing forward. In fact, most learning theory in the twentieth and twenty-first centuries has been an effort to collapse Descartes's split: Dewey's pragmatism attempted such a unification (Dewey 1933, 1938, 1956; Mead 1964/1932; Popkewitz 2001), as did Lev Vygotsky's notions of language and society (Vygostky 1978), Jean Piaget's theory of cognitive equilibration (Piaget 1954), and most versions of constructivism (Cobb 1994; Fosnot 1996).

Knowledge is best viewed as a process not a product, and individuals make meaning through a negotiated interpretation of experience inside personalized constructs (coming from previous life experiences), contextual positionings (coming from the embedded sociopolitical relationships that mark any context), and their social interactions with others (and the language that facilitates these interactions). Meaning-making exists as a dialectic among self, other(s), situation, and purpose(s)—and means that knowledge is always a holistic, continuous, and recursively constructed assemblage of past and present, personal and professional, stance and understanding.

Eastern Notions of Knowledge

Eastern philosophy conceives of knowledge very differently and in ways that recommend a more ecological formulation.[3] Rather than viewing knowledge through the linear, binary lens that Greek (and later, European Continental) philosophy used, Eastern thinkers have traditionally embraced a more holistic, less linear conception of knowledge that views meaning as wider and rounder than the narrow frame of "reason" or "intellect." Harmony, not understanding, is the intent. In approximately the sixth century BC, Lao-tzu taught that the "way of life" (tao) is beyond reason—that wisdom (or *enlightenment* as it might more accurately be termed) consists of a deep appreciation for the interconnectedness of all things, for the value of the present, and for the insignificant role of the individual inside the more important, all-inclusive web of the "Nameless Reality" (Kornfield 1993).

This Eastern strand of influence is significant here not only for providing a counterweight to offset the linear logocentrism of Western philosophy concerning knowledge, but also because several educational thinkers have incorporated pieces of this more holistic conception of knowledge into their theories of teacher knowledge. Emphases on the present, on resisting boundaries and categories, and on acute awareness are all Taoist tenets found in some current conceptions of teacher knowledge. Robert Tremmel (1993) has used Zen Buddhism to reconceptualize teacher reflection by foregrounding the present, the simultaneous, and the holistic in how teachers might think about their practice. James Moffett's Buddhist beliefs sometimes emerged in his professional work as he reconceptualized relationships between people and ideas within learning (Moffett 1992, 1994). Donald Schön's (1987) theory of reflection-in-action offers an implicit (and probably inadvertent) nod to Buddhism, when it eliminates distinctions between knowing and acting to instead posit a simultaneous, seamless process of considering phenomena, formulating theory, and acting. These holistic framings support a focus on *identity* as the unit of analysis within human development and professional learning; this book's conclusion offers more on this.

The notion that knowledge consists of more than simply what can be intellectually grasped or linearly represented has played an important, if minority, role in Western research on what a teacher should "know," and from where this knowledge emerges. In fact, Fred Korthagen and Jos Kessels's (1999) use of "gestalt" in teacher learning (discussed later in this chapter) reflects this very conception. These ideas help form the understanding that knowledge must be defined broadly, ö that learning must be seen to include all parts of one's experience, and that knowledge is inextricably linked to context.

Cognitive and Situated Theories of Learning

At the center of the topic of learning-to-teach is the question of whether knowledge is constructed in context or acquired in the abstract. From this question, entire conceptions—and their subsequent programs—of teacher knowledge spin out as each answer becomes an elaborated, articulated theory of practice. Dewey's characterizations of theory and practice and his subsequent consolidation of laboratory and apprenticeship models are one such theory (Dewey 1904, 1933). Lee Shulman's introduction and analysis of pedagogical content knowledge would be another (Shulman 1986a, 1987; Grossman 1990; Wilson, Shulman, and Richert 1987). Jean Lave and Etienne Wenger's "Legitimate Peripheral Participation" is a third (Lave and Wenger 1991). Methodologically, these analyses are both epistemological and cognitive because, fundamentally, the question of whether knowledge is constructed in context or acquired in the abstract is both epistemological and cognitive. If epistemology is the study of the *nature of knowledge* ("What is the thing known?") and cognition is the study of *knowing* ("What is the relationship of knower to thing known?"), then any thorough examination of teacher learning includes them both.

The debate about whether learning is situated or cognitive is profound and long-standing.[4] At its center lies a dispute over whether the primary unit of analysis within learning is the individual or the social collective (Anderson et al. 2000; Cobb and Bowers 1999; Lave 1988; Lave and Wenger 1991; Putnam and Borko 2000). The cognitive tradition locates learning inside *internal cognitive processes*—in other words, information-processing mechanisms inside the individual, which are believed to connect external stimuli with individual responses. This cognitive perspective does not ignore the role of context (or its synonym *environment*) but views context—or "task and relevant features of the setting" (Cobb and Bowers 1999)—as existing independently of situation and purpose and acting as *influence on* learning.

On the other side, because reaction to what they believe is an overly narrow treatment of learning and context, one that, they argue, deemphasizes roles of affect, context, culture, and history, several researchers began instead to view learning as occurring *firmly inside* an interaction between individual and environment (Greeno 1997; Lave 1988; Lave and Wenger 1991). These social theorists put forward a situated perspective: a view of learning that takes as primary unit of analysis an "interactive system composed of groups of individuals together with the material and representational resources they use" (Cobb and Bowers 1999, 5). Here, learning is perceived entirely as a social activity within an actual context in which participants begin to think in new ways, undergo identity shifts, adopt new ways of using language, reformulate relationships to the world, and produce both artifacts and memories. Lave and Wenger write that such a perspective of learning presumes

> that there is no activity that is not situated. It impl[ies] emphasis on comprehensive understanding involving the whole person rather than "receiving" a body of factual knowledge about the world; on activity in and with the world; and on the view that agent, activity, and the world mutually constitute each other. (Lave and Wenger 1991, 33)

Though both sides (except for extremists at each end) agree that learning is a process of constructing a new thing out of available materials, the cognitive perspective treats knowledge as an entity, whereas the situated perspective treats it as an activity. In fact, the differences between them are reducible to a single question: "How closely or loosely is knowledge tied to the context in which it was constructed?" (Ammon 2000). The cognitive perspective presumes knowledge can be constructed within one context yet unproblematically employed in another context. The situated perspective assumes that, because knowledge and context inextricably relate, knowledge does not transfer but rather is reconstructed anew each time.

Traditionally, these two competing perspectives—and the tension between them—have structured the theories, research, and policies of teacher education in North America. Those who presume learning is primarily cognitive could accept, for example, a definition of teacher knowledge as proved theory taught to beginning teachers and applied appropriately by those teachers to classroom situations (e.g., Eliot, characterized in Lagemann 2000; Thorndike, characterized in Kliebard 1995). Such a theoretical view undergirds the loosely assembled bundle of conceptions, curricula, and sequence considered the mainstream model of twentieth-century teacher education in the United States: Pre-service teachers learn theories and teaching approaches in university classrooms for a semester and then try out and internalize those theories in some kind of supervised teaching practicum. For most of the last fifty years, this has been a dominant model of teacher education. This programmatic approach, though, rests on two shaky theoretical premises: that learning takes place primarily in the mind of the individual learner, and that knowledge transfers relatively intact.

If, instead, we accept that the process of teacher learning is often situated, then it means we presume that teachers construct their own knowledge. This means, then, that a teacher's ways of knowing are inextricably linked to his or her lived experience(s). If we grant this, it follows that we must view each teacher as a unique and three-dimensional learner—someone who combines life, learning, and practice to create individual understandings of, and relationships to, the world and him- or herself. Epistemologically speaking, who one is as a *person* affects who one is as both a *learner* and a *teacher*. Life and learning intertwine. Such a view is often invoked to defend teacher education approaches that stress problem-posing curricula, communities of practice, and an emphasis on pre-service teachers acknowledging their personal influences (Darling-Hammond 1994; Dewey 1904, 1933; Freire 1970; Putnam and Borko 2000; Schön 1987). This approach rests on the premises that (1) learning takes place within the whole person always acting inside a unique setting, and (2) knowledge is inextricably linked to context. It is at times criticized for allowing students' own naive learner theories to dominate learning, or for encouraging excessive "navel gazing." And it is sometimes criticized for a determinism that presumes that people are prisoners of their experience.

That is the dichotomous version of this debate. And, oddly, participants in the theoretical debate rarely posit legitimate places between these two extremes (though see Anderson et al. 2000 for one such place). To examine learning in ways both deep and broad, I choose to accept that, separately, each perspective illuminates a fundamental, though different, aspect of learning and, together, both perspectives complement each other to illuminate the conditions under which external stimuli guide human development. It appears fair to say that all knowledge is to some extent bounded by context, yet it is that degree of "boundedness" that separates the two perspectives. As we think about teacher education, we should strive to strike an accurate, useful balance. Too much abstraction makes knowledge difficult to apply in the classroom, yet too much contextualization makes knowledge difficult to apply in the face of unpredictable situations of practice. Cognitive perspectives highlight individuals acquiring (semi-)discrete skills and concepts, whereas situated perspectives highlight ways social activities organize and shape new understandings. Taken together, the complementary contributions of both perspectives should prove valuable. John Anderson et al. (2000) write:

> A more complete *cognitive theory* will include more specific explanations of differences between learning environments, considered as effects of different contexts, and a more complete *situative theory* will include more specific explanations of individual students' proficiencies and understandings, considered as their participation in interactions with each other and with material and socially constructed conceptual systems. (Anderson et al. 2000, 12; italics added.)

In many university-based teacher preparation programs, the dominant model of teacher learning still largely relies on and puts forward (consciously or not) a cognitive conception of learning. In practice it most often takes the form of teacher educators delivering their interpretations of established, often university-generated, theories of learning and teaching, prescriptive strategies for classroom instruction, and the occasional added-on space for practitioner reflection. Student teachers are then presumed to practice and internalize the approaches they are taught in their classroom practica, guided by experienced teachers and university supervisors charged with somehow assisting the student teachers to mediate the university theories into classroom practices. This tacit reliance on knowledge transfer, and its attendant underacknowledgment of situated perspectives, appear to be misaligned with how teachers actually learn to teach.

Accepting such a stance toward learning leads many university teacher education programs, intentionally or not, to officially prescribe (through program organization and curricula) and unofficially inscribe (through embedded conceptions and practices of faculties and cooperating teachers) an approach that in the aggregate presumes (1) teaching theory is primarily university theory, (2) knowledge transfers directly, (3) preservice teachers directly internalize what is presented to them, and (4) context is separable from learning. This misalignment could account for why teacher education so often proves to be a weak interruption in the development of teachers (Cuban 1990, 1993; Lortie 1975; Rust 1994; Wideen, Mayer-Smith, and Moon 1998; Zeichner and Tabachnick 1981). It might also explain why so many practicing teachers dismiss university teacher education as hollow theory and empty administrative hoops to jump through, and why beginning teachers often have difficulty reconciling the infamous theory-practice split in education (Hoffman-Kipp and Olsen 2007).

Defining Teacher Knowledge: A Move Toward the Holistic

Teacher knowledge, especially by practitioners, administrators, and the public, is often defined narrowly—hyperrationally or overly mentalist, to be precise. To check this, consider asking an educator what teacher knowledge is. This person will generally presume it consists of what a teacher intellectually "knows" about subject matter, teaching, learning, and classroom management. The answer will probably include established theories of teaching and child psychology the person was taught, regularities of school and classroom contexts, and something about subject matter knowledge—surely concrete methods of pedagogy, classroom management, and lesson planning would be mentioned. We can consider this bundle of conceptions as primarily university or otherwise published conceptions and skills teachers are expected to learn and apply to classroom situations. Donald Schön (1987) names this body of understanding and skills "technical rationality." Maybe the respondent would also cite various concrete lessons-from-inside-the-classroom; for example, that in order to prevent squeaking, one should break a new stick of chalk before using it or an exhortation to keep an eye on that student leaning back in her chair, because she is about to disrupt the classroom. Or, of course, that perennial schoolteacher adage: Do not smile before winter break. This second category can be categorized as experience-based lessons of effective teaching; Lee Shulman terms it "wisdom of practice" (Shulman 1986a). Both, however, are primarily mental understandings of and/or technical approaches to teaching and learning.

However, if we are to accept that knowledge construction is situated, it follows that knowledge derives from more than cognitive understandings and technical skills. It includes multiple layers of context and social interactions. Similarly, if teacher learning is a holistic process that incorporates several aspects of a teacher's life, then we should widen our conception of teacher knowledge. Knowledge does not reside solely in the abstract, intellectual mind of a teacher but requires the whole person. In this book, teacher knowledge has been defined widely to include those aspects traditionally circumscribed within traditional definitions of teacher knowledge, but also a teacher's values, goals, dispositions, memories, changing identities, personality aspects, physical being, emotions, and political ideologies. Because all these factors enter into a teacher's process of interpreting, considering, and enacting teaching, it seems illogical to exclude them and their products from any definition of teacher knowledge. This wider framing encourages us to treat teacher learning more ecologically, and as less fixed.

The Construction of Teacher Knowledge: Presenting a New Model

The research on which this book is based uncovered a process whereby a beginning teacher combines professional theories and the wisdom of practice with those personal dispositions, conceptions, feelings, goals, and memories to construct an always developing understanding of and approach toward teaching. It is as if these nontechnical, nonspecialized influences (themselves deriving from lived experience set inside nested layers of context) sit alongside formal teacher learning, yet are constantly (and automatically, and often unconsciously) invoked and used as knowledge is constructed. For example, a pre-service teacher is exposed to some theory or technical approach about teaching: say, Piaget's stage model of cognitive development in children—we will call this theory "A." This new learning stimulus travels through the range of prior and present influences—call this collection of influences "B." And the formal theory (Piaget's developmentalism here) is confirmed or denied, accepted or rejected, adjusted and shaped to fit with the teacher's previous conception of the world (coming from those B influences) inside the particular context of the moment (call this "C"), and the result is a uniquely constructed piece of teacher knowledge—a personalized understanding of and approach to teaching. Really, this knowledge is an understanding of *one individual's contextualized* version of Piaget's constructivism—one that may or may not accurately reflect constructivism as Piaget imagined it, or as the education professor/program intended to present it.

If we refer to this resulting piece of teacher knowledge (this pre-service teacher's understanding of constructivism) as "TK," then in a way we have a logical equation: A + B + C = TK:

(A)		(B)		(C)	(TK)
formal	$\leftrightarrow$	informal prior and	$\leftrightarrow$	current situation =	teacher knowledge[5]
theory		current influences			
and/or					
approach					

This is an important conception, because it differs from the classical, knowledge transfer conception: one we could represent as A = TK. It also differs from the situated conception, one that foregrounds context; that view might be (oversimplistically) represented as A + C = TK.

Another way of describing this process is to use the analogy of the "cut-and-paste" function within word processing software. A writer sometimes "cuts" or copies one or more pieces of text from existing documents and stores them temporarily in her software program's "clipboard." Then, as she constructs her new document, she can insert the relevant text from the clipboard into the current document. In this way, she uses the information and ideas from previous documents to create new ones. Past and present combine to form something uniquely relevant to the particular context. Consider this metaphor within the process of learning to teach: The clipboard is that space, that virtual chamber of past and informal influences, that is always loaded and instantly available—and the learner cuts and pastes relevant pieces of the stored "text" onto the current situation to form a personalized, contextualized product. A piece of knowledge, then, is the product of at least three influences: past texts, a present interpretation of the situation, and the new stimuli that initiated the process.[6]

Let me operationalize the clipboard metaphor using some actual data. One of the secondary English teachers in the study, Liz, was exposed to the familiar product-versus-process debate in literacy instruction in her program in two simultaneous ways. One was a reading assignment, class discussion, and exchange with her curriculum and instruction professor about traditional teaching models, and the second was a discussion about product versus process in her methods seminar. We can view these two events as the stimulus that initiated the writing of a new "text." As Liz began developing her new understanding—began writing this new text—she found herself in a quandary: She interpreted both professors as being very critical of the product approach to teaching and felt they were instructing her to always privilege student understandings, yet her own ideas about teaching English, stemming, she revealed, in large part from her traditional English teacher father (whom she admired professionally and personally) and her own memories from school, were decidedly product-oriented. Her prior conception held that students learn from disciplinary expert teachers instructing them. Specifically, she was having trouble sacrificing the teacher-as-expert notion she felt was embedded in a product approach. She felt both professors were pushing an "all-students-are-experts" conception shrouded in a process approach to teaching. And she believed that if the students were experts, the teacher could not be expert. In the following passage she describes a verbal exchange she and her professor had in class the day before:

> At the same time, and what I tried to say yesterday, which I don't think I did well, and I don't think I'll be permitted to, is that the teacher ought to be an expert on his subject. And there's a reason that we have people who are experts on their subject and why an English teacher has a different educational background than a science teacher. It's not because he facilitates [discussions] in a specific way, it's because he's got information, he's got training, and he's managed to synthesize things in an academic

fashion that the science teacher doesn't do and vice versa. That's why he's the English teacher, and that's why I go to him for the English class, instead of to my homeroom teacher who's the gym teacher. And that fact should not be lost.

And I actually felt, until other people said things which were remotely in agreement with what I was saying, I really felt like she was just, you know, yelling at me. Not yelling, but I definitely felt, like, slugged.
BRAD: You think she was attacking you?
LIZ: I think she was really defensive.

Not only was there a difference of opinion, but Liz's hurt feelings (call it losing face [Goffman 1959], or an asymmetrical standoff between two people's cultural capital [Bourdieu 1991], or a sudden shift in power/knowledge [Foucault 1977]) disposed her to be less accepting of this professor's ideas in the future.

Simultaneously, Liz was grappling with a recurring conversation she and her girlfriend were having in which Liz would listen to her girlfriend tell tragic tales of hating high school English:

For [her], school was a really big problem, and it's really important for me to see that and to hear that. Partly, it's just like, I know how much her insecurities about her language ability and her grammar and her ability to communicate and be articulate were just like a cloud over her. I don't know what happened, but for some reason that wasn't good. So, I definitely have that in mind, to keep an eye on that. I think understanding that has really made me less of an elitist.

This influence from her girlfriend's past encouraged her to reevaluate her father's method of teaching (which she had complimented during our first interview) in light of those students who do not succeed, who find, for example, grammar very difficult and are made to feel insecure in class. Liz said:

I guess in some ways I'm finding out my dad wasn't the greatest teacher. Actually, what my dad is really good at is teaching the smart class and teaching the AP classes and teaching the kids who are already there and adding to what they know and giving them technical skills and fine-tuning them. I think the kids who need it fall to the back of the room, and that is a way that my dad is not a great teacher. My brother who is in his early thirties now has friends who are his own age who were my dad's students. And one who is smart and bright. And another—or the sister

of another—is like, "Oh, your dad's Mister Mason? He made me feel like
I was nothing."

These prior influences, current relationships, and affective dispositions
were combining with the formal teacher theory she was expected to learn,
and the resulting space—or "text," thus far—became characterized by
the uncertainty, uniqueness, and value conflicts that Schön (1987) argues
render "technical rationality" insufficient. Liz's learning was no direct
internalization of university theory. As Liz created her understanding, she
automatically drew on previous texts using this virtual "clipboard."

At this point in the chronological sequence of Liz's assembly of the
product-versus-process debate, a new variable was introduced that allowed her a way out: a reading assignment from Lisa Delpit's (1995) *Other
People's Children.* In the following interview passage, Liz uses Delpit (and
two separate personal memories it invoked) to legitimize and therefore
retain her belief in a teacher-as-expert approach to teaching grammar.
Her particular understanding of Delpit[7] allowed her to preserve a belief
that the teacher is the expert who tells students how to speak and write
but, because she locates this belief inside an interpretation of Delpit
viewing direct instruction as aiding, not injuring, students, Liz can jet-
tison her fear that she will damage the self-esteem of students like her
girlfriend or that former one of her dad's:

> [Delpit] did this great thing in the beginning [of her essay "The Silenced
> Dialogue"], which was something like—I found out that a child can learn
> from being constantly corrected, and not end up fucked-up, or something
> like that. I was babysitting for a friend's kid last night, and he's ten years
> old. The father came home, and we were playing [the word game] Boggle.
> Adults playing Boggle—it's not like kids playing Boggle. You know, we're
> getting words, and the kid is trying so hard, and it's clear how frustrated
> he's getting, because he doesn't see anything, and we're just writing away.
> He comes up with four words and a couple of them were four or five let-
> ters, but they are all misspelled, and he didn't get the points. And I could
> see how hard that was for him. I can remember being that kid for whom
> it was so hard. I really wanted to play a game with my parents, but they're
> playing with each other, and I'd try to play, but you can't even be in the
> conversation, because you're just so far apart in terms of ability. So I know
> how frustrating that is, but I also know that I had something to aspire to.
> Because I had to play by adult rules, I knew how not to spell things. And
> I actually have memories of things I misspelled, and knowing that they
> were wrong, and I won't do that again.

The resulting set of understandings, values, and conceptions—this piece of her teacher knowledge, this epistemological "text"—will, for a while at least, guide her thoughts and actions about teaching, grammar, Delpit, literacy, and her program instructors as she continues her teacher development. It was constructed as a negotiation among formal learning stimuli; invoked informal relationships, contexts, and values; and various linked memories of past experiences.

It is this collection of past and present, personal and informal influences—this clipboard of general dispositions, feelings, goals, and memories—that constitutes teacher knowledge as it ought to be conceived. Freema Elbaz (1981) and Jean Clandinin (1985) use the term *images* to describe the deeply embedded cognitive schemata teachers use to organize, process, or attach meaning to new concepts or experiences. They argue that these images act both as filters that adjust the new information to fit into the teacher's already existing worldview and as metaphors that serve as containers shaping the organization and representation of the knowledge held. Fred Korthagen and Jos Kessels (1999) borrow the German psychological term *Gestalt* to refer to the "holistic unity" of all influences—including past experiences, feelings, personal values, and role conceptions—on a teacher that are at once triggered by a classroom situation. They mention that they prefer the term *gestalt* over *image* because it is less vague and less connotative of the visual sense.

Following Korthagen and Kessels, I use the term *gestalt* to get at this place where prior and present, formal and informal, cognitive and affective experiences are actively used as knowledge is constructed. It is a mediating place in between the influences on learning-to-teach and the resulting teacher knowledge. This means that learning is not the direct acquisition and internalization of information received from elsewhere but is rather an indirect, mediated, more recursive process where a learner automatically processes new information by placing it up against the gestalt space of influences and allowing for a reciprocal adjustment of both sides. The new information will be rejected, accepted, adjusted, or interpreted *in relation to* the learner's prior conceptions of the particular information, the larger context of its relevance, and even of the world in general. And the prior conceptions will also be adjusted—whether by revising memories and previous values or by a conscious reframing of one's previously held worldview. Graphically, the relationship among components might look like Figure 1.1 below.

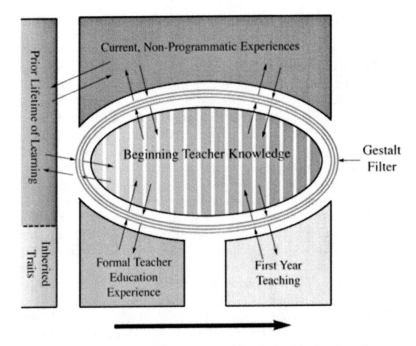

Figure 1.1 **The Knowledge Process of Beginning Teacher Learning**

The Role of Prior Knowledge

If we accept the process of learning described previously, then prior knowledge must play a significant role as a teaching candidate learns to teach. Several researchers have posited that pre-service teachers begin the process of learning to teach already in possession of powerful conceptions of teaching, learning, and classrooms they picked up from prior experiences (e.g., Britzman 1986, 1991; Calderhead 1988; Elbaz 1981; Feiman-Nemser and Buchmann 1985; Kagan 1992; Knowles 1992; Quiocho and Rios 2000; Weinstein 1989).

Beginning teachers process formal teacher knowledge—that "traditional conception" of teacher knowledge discussed earlier—by combining it with their personal conceptions (really, those memories, understandings, identities, values, and dispositions that make up a worldview or identity) in their gestalt. The formal knowledge can pass through the gestalt relatively unaltered: I call this a *confirmatory* learning experience. Or it can be wholly rejected by the understandings in the gestalt, what I call a *disconfirmatory* learning experience. A third option is that the learner takes part of the new information (in or out of context, interpreted as intended or interpreted very differently) and attaches it to his or her gestalt such that the new product becomes a prior conception strengthened or altered by this new information, this new "learning." This scenario I call an *appropriating* learning experience. For example, Liz interpreted Delpit differently than did her professors, so she could retain her product-based understanding of teaching grammar and reject the process-based approach of both her methods and curriculum professors. This is both a disconfirmatory experience (she rejected the programmatic conception because it did not confirm her previously held understandings) and an appropriating experience (she used pieces of the programmatic conception, interpreted as she wished, in constructing her new understanding).

There exists a complex range of ways in which—and conditions under which—the new (formal) teacher knowledge combines with the preexisting (personal) knowledge construct. Reconceptualizing learning-to-teach by illuminating and understanding this holistic knowledge (or identity) process exists as the primary endeavor for teacher preparation researchers. It is a challenge that I hope will be taken up using this newer, situated, holistic framing of knowledge and learning-to-teach rather than continuing to rely on antiquated, overly intellectual, linear notions of knowledge and teacher learning. Chapter two examines this professional learning process in more detail.

Notes

1. There is a politics of teacher knowledge occurring here as well as an epistemology of teacher knowledge. As much as reconceptualizations of teacher knowledge are about descriptive views of knowledge, they are also ideological attempts at reallocating power. The implicit question embedded in discussions like this one is "Who owns the knowledge?" See Cochran-Smith and Lytle (1999) and Apple (1999). Also consider feminist literature such as that of Simone de Beauvoir (1952), Mary Belenky et al. (1986), Betty Friedan (1963), bell hooks (1993), and Carol Gilligan (1982).

2. This concept is similar to Piaget's "conservatism of knowledge" (Gruber and Voneche 1977).

3. It is misleading to suggest that all Eastern religions share one coherent set of beliefs, although they do share several ontological principles. Here, I rely on Taoism and Buddhism, because they are the Eastern religions that most influenced the research on teacher knowledge I have read.

4. It is sometimes termed as a debate between *individual* and *social* perspectives (Anderson et al. 2000). Additionally, the situated perspective is sometimes discussed in relation to "sociocultural learning theory" (Oakes and Lipton 2003).

5. It is worth mentioning that this process of construction iteratively loops back and forth on itself as each element is shaped and reshaped by others. This linear equation is merely a heuristic.

6. And the phrase "piece of knowledge," as it suggests a discrete fragment separable from others, of course belies my ecological intent to view phenomena holistically and in continuous construction. This phrasing is merely rhetorical to make my description of the process clear.

7. An interpretation different from that of both her professors, and one from which, most likely, even Delpit would distance herself.

2

Liz
One Beginner Assembles a Teacher Self

[I am] A learner with the simplest, a teacher of the thoughtfullest;
A novice beginning, yet experient of myriads of seasons;
Of every hue and caste am I, of every rank and religion;
I exist as I am—that is enough;
Do I contradict myself?
Very well, then, I contradict myself;
(I am large—I contain multitudes.)
—*Walt Whitman*

LIZ: One of the things I've noticed that's made me not so thrilled with teaching is that I don't really like my behavior.

BRAD: What do you mean?

LIZ: I'm doing the things I never thought I'd do.

BRAD: Like what?

LIZ: Just the way I react to kids, the things that piss me off. Getting kind of, you know, snotty with kids.... When I get angry with a class it's because I'm trying to hold them to a particular tautness, and they won't—it won't work. Because it's my feeling that for kids to be on task they need to be on task, need order. They need to be focused. And it's my job to keep them focused. When I can't keep a class focused, or when those kids refuse, I can pull, and I can pull in as hard as I want, but I'm going to break the string before they get it. Before they straighten up. And so I had to make a decision: Am I going to keep pulling and kicking kids out and having, you know, what could be mutiny—and what's *been* mutiny? Or do I try and relax a little bit and hope for as much as I can get? And I went for the

31

latter, which means that less gets done and there's a little bit more chaos, but there's less mutiny.

—From my final interview with Liz

Grappling with Models of Teaching

Like any teacher—like any person—Liz is a complex bundle of influences, beliefs, values, features, perceptions, and conceptions. She is wide and contains multitudes. This bundle of pieces, modernly called a "self,"[1] appears by surface glance to be autonomous and categorizable: Liz is a white woman from a middle-class background in Staten Island, New York, who is in her late twenties, college-educated, quasi-confident, idealistic, able to crack a joke, naturally self-deprecating, the daughter of two teachers, and someone who loves rock music. Available research might cast her as a typical teacher candidate (Hargreaves 1995; Lanier and Little 1986; Lortie 1975; Wideen, Mayer-Smith, and Moon 1998). Yet, having spent four years studying Liz—analyzing her ways of teaching, thinking, talking, acting—I found that she is, of course, unique.

The story of Liz's teacher development is, in large part, a story of Liz fashioning a coherent body of teacher knowledge from myriad experiences, memories, and relationships. Chapter one addresses theoretical connections between learning and lived experience, presenting a holistic view of development as resulting from identity negotiations among multiple sources and ways of interpreting the world. The notion of coherence—the ordering and assembling of those sources and conceptions to form a balanced whole—I briefly take up now. From sources as varied as Lao-tzu to Aristotle, Freud to de Beauvoir, Hemingway to Heidegger comes discussion of the human attempt for an individual to create and maintain a stable self, to more or less coherently align the various parts that produce meaning. Charlotte Linde (1993) calls this "the creation of coherence."

If the pieces are misaligned, the self is presumed to fall out of equilibrium into disharmony (Campbell 1988, 1991). Chinese medicine uses chi and the balance metaphor of yin and yang (Kaptchuck 1983; Zhing-yi, Yuan-zhu, and Xuan-du 1978). Freudian psychoanalysis—borrowing from German embryology (Waddington 1956)—adopted the metaphor of a blocked stream that must be thrown open before the water again flows healthily (Gardner 1993; Lakoff 1990). Leon Festinger (1957) coined the term *cognitive dissonance* to describe the discomfort of simultaneously possessing irreconcilable ideas. The hermeneutic tradition within Continental philosophy (Heidegger 1927, through Gamadar 1985, and Taylor 1985) maintains that we humans are our own projects, each of us continually interpreting and reinterpreting those beliefs, activities, future plans, and relationships in which we are engaged in order to construct a functional self. Epistemologically speaking, as Liz naturally (and automatically) strove for coherence in assembling those understandings I call her *teacher identity,* she manipulated, juxtaposed, and fastened bundles of professional and personal interpretations, identities, memories, and ways of knowing into something she considered (consciously or not) coherent. She was fashioning a teacher self.

In this chapter I focus on one central issue that emerged throughout Liz's knowledge construction: her grappling with competing models of teaching within *the student-centered-teaching versus didactic-teaching debate.* This struggle structured the emergence of Liz's teacher self. By organizing an analysis around this facet of Liz's professional development, I examine the various knowledge and identity patterns in play, follow the patterns and their mediating interrelationships across sources of influence, and present a holistic epistemological perspective within the constraints of two-dimensional prose. The discussion intends to accomplish four simultaneous objectives: (1) to chronicle Liz's teacher development as a process narrative, (2) to empirically illustrate the model of professional knowledge construction introduced in the previous chapter, (3) to emphasize holistic relationships among knowledge influences, and (4) to illustrate the *chronological* development of Liz as a teacher without neglecting the *iterative* epistemological process of teacher identity.

Competing Models of Teaching

It is no surprise to realize there exists a multitude of models for teaching. I define a "model of teaching" as a more or less coherent bundle of teaching features and conceptions that stands as both a conceptual and methodological representation of one approach to teaching. These models are sometimes described as *metaphors* for teaching.[2] Sometimes they are recognized and treated explicitly; more often they are implicitly presumed, only to be uncovered by looking closely at behavior and language use. Some models of teaching emerge from film or television: Robin Williams's teacher-as-entertainer in *Dead Poets Society*; Edward James Olmos's tough-love-comedian rendering of Jaime Escalante in *Stand and Deliver*; and any of the young, committed, multicultural warriors ("warrior"—an interesting metaphor of its own) from the once-popular television program *Boston Public*. Other models of teaching can be found in print: from newspaper articles characterizing teachers as unionized professionals or beleaguered missionaries, routinized incompetents or underprepared victims, to the ubiquitous Sunday feature on that innovative teacher with the interesting background (e.g., *The New York Times Magazine*, 1998). These iconized portraits of teachers serve a complicated purpose within an audience's commonsense understandings of teaching, because they are meant both to embody the audience's preconceptions about teaching and, simultaneously, to adjust those conceptions into new ones. These models become employed and recycled because they efficiently signal more complex bundles of recognized phenomena, even as they reify and adjust the very phenomena upon which they intend to rely (Fiske 1992).

Though most educators try to be careful when employing generalizations, treating teaching in metaphorical terms has its value. For example, if we talk about a teacher as a technician, we are able to import prior understandings of technicians into the domain of teaching (e.g., skill-oriented, procedure-based, competent, standardized). One can also more easily communicate or comprehend complex collections of features by reducing and putting a recognizable shape on them; a generalization offers a preexisting schema on which one can hang new, related ideas; plus, it allows a relative newcomer to appear veteran by using a shorthand language that invokes complex theories.

Within expert domains of education research, teacher education, and school policy, we find an abundance of metaphors for teaching in use: teacher-as-technician, teacher-as-manager, teaching-as-art, teacher-as-learner, teacher-as-content-delivery-person, teacher-as-friend, teacher-as-activist. Each of these bundled conceptions of teaching acts both as a *resulting shape of* thinking and acting and as an *actual influence on* thinking and acting. For example, Jean Clandinin (1985) presents a case study of a teacher whose metaphor (Clandinin prefers the term *image*) of teaching as "running a house" gives shape to her teaching knowledge. This image allows the teacher to neatly collect her desires to connect home to classroom, personal life to professional life, her childhood to the lives of her students, her view of teacher as nurturer. The notion of teaching as running a house embodies her knowledge of teaching and highlights affective, personal, and moral components of teaching as well as the more traditional curricular, pedagogical, and intellectual ones. And yet, this use of a metaphor for teaching must also hold unintended influence over her knowledge of teaching and learning. If she conceives of teaching as running a house, then surely there are facets of "house" that unwittingly carry over to "classroom." We might presume that she places a high premium on students cleaning up after themselves, or that she sets a maternal climate, or that her own ideas about competition among siblings affect her ideas about competition among students. It could be hypothesized that she sees her students (regardless of their cultural backgrounds) as versions of her own children or herself as a child. George Lakoff and Mark Turner (1989) write:

> For the same reasons that schemas and metaphors give us power to conceptualize and reason, so they have power over us. Anything that we rely on constantly, unconsciously, and automatically is so much part of us that it cannot be easily resisted, in large measure because it is barely even noticed. (63)

As I studied Liz's development, it became clear that she was considering and experimenting with several models of teaching: from the *teacher-as-cool-friend* model of her own "hippest, jeans-wearing English teacher" in tenth grade, on whom she "had a crush," to her *teacher-as-expert* English teacher father who "believes in kids sitting in rows facing the teacher" and is "flabbergasted" that Liz's credentialing program employs group learning: "But why are you paying tuition to listen to the kid next to you? He doesn't know any more than you do. It's the professor you're paying for." From the *student-centered/cooperative learning teacher* model her credentialing program espoused—"It's the emerging paradigm," one professor told me—to the *teacher-as-technician* model her favorite Casals University professor embodied and advocated, or the *teacher-as-agent-of-social-change* Liz's family instilled in her: "[Teaching] was this noble thing to do in our family."

Her (rarely conscious) manipulation of these various models of teaching allowed Liz to make use of the many strands of teacher knowledge: to automatically organize, compare, eliminate, adjust, and ultimately assemble knowledge content from diverse sources into a relatively coherent body of professional understandings. Examining these scores of places in the data—these instances where Liz relied upon shared, shorthand conceptions of teaching—reveals useful information about her knowledge influences and how she conceived of them.

Liz's Assembly of the Student-Centered Versus Teacher-Centered Teacher Debate

Part One: Initial Conceptions

A primary knowledge struggle for Liz was the interpretation, evaluation, and assembly of the *student-centered-versus-teacher-centered continuum* within teaching. This education topic is a tension that has endured for more than a century, beginning with European educationalists like Pestalozzi, Montessori, and Froebel (Cremin, Shannon, and Townsend 1954) and capturing the attention of turn-of-the-century U.S. theorists such as Hall, Thorndike, Eliot, and Dewey (Kliebard 1995) before embedding itself into part of most every succeeding generation of education debate—from lecturing-versus-group-work controversies and phonics-versus-whole-language battles to the relative merits of computer-aided instruction or class size reduction. On the "student-centered" side are developmentalists, humanists, and constructivists who emphasize the student as the center of the curriculum and argue that a teacher should—to paraphrase Herbert Kliebard quoting John Dewey—first discover each child's own "urgent impulses and habits" and then, by supplying the proper environment, direct them "in a fruitful and orderly way" toward discovery (Kliebard 1995; Lagemann 2000). The motivation for learning, Dewey argued, will take care of itself (Dewey 1902).

On the "teacher-centered"—or "traditional" or "didactic"—side of the debate are mental disciplinarians, social efficiency theorists, and direct instruction advocates, who believe, instead, that all pupils should be taught in the same way and to the same extent, and who encourage primary emphasis on the teacher who delivers information to students and leads them in drills designed to reinforce internalization of that information (Delpit 1995; Kliebard 1995; National Education Association 1993; Ravitch 2000). Of course, the debate in actual practice is rarely as polarized as this gloss pretends. Most teachers and researchers of teaching conceive of this tension as a broad space in which effective practice lies somewhere in between the extremes. It is important to note that Liz was familiar with none of this history.

In the remaining pages of this chapter, I use Liz's assembly of the debate to illustrate the myriad knowledge sources at play and their interrelationships as Liz continuously formed and re-formed her teacher identity. *She framed the student-centered-versus-teacher-centered debate as a binary continuum, as a more or less zero-sum game between, primarily, her credentialing program as model and her father as model.* A central theme in Liz's knowledge construction concerns her belief that student-centered teaching and teacher-centered teaching exist at opposite poles of a linear spectrum and to lean in one direction necessarily sacrifices the other. Much of her prior understanding of teaching derived from her father, and when she spoke of her father's teaching, she often employed the teacher-as-expert model—a conception that Liz set in direct opposition to the student-centered-teacher model she believed represented the Casals ideal. Her father had just retired after teaching English for thirty-five years in several New York City public and private high schools. Liz reported that he always loved teaching and considered himself good at it; she also mentioned that he was known and respected in the field and had written a published grammar book. Discussing her father as teacher, she tended to group together a cluster of teaching models: the traditional teacher, the teacher as expert, the teacher who succeeds primarily with academically motivated students (and disappoints the remainder), and the satisfied professional at the end of a successful career.

These teaching features, bundled together, came to represent for Liz two related but different notions. One is that it stood for her father as primary knowledge source, a container of conceptions that had great, but complex, influence on her own developing ideas about teaching. And the second is that it became Liz's model for the traditional, teacher-centered teacher and all that entailed. Liz told me,

My father believes in kids sitting in rows or perhaps in a horseshoe; in either form they face the teacher. My father believes that the teacher has the information. That's why he's the teacher. Groups may make kids less shy, more expressive, but inevitably they collapse into social discussions. What's worse, he says, they don't prepare kids for what they'll see in college.

Frequently Liz discussed her dad as a good, satisfied, professional teacher whom she admires:

> And you know, thinking about it now, or recently as I have, you know, my dad was a good teacher. And he seemed always to have been a good teacher ... he stuck to the text ... students were able to understand [and] enjoy things that they read. I think he was very good in discussion, kind of doing that switchback [with students] ... like, "Okay, so you're saying—" or, "What did you mean by—" or, "Okay, how do you respond to so-and-so?" And making good insights on the fly, which is something I hope to get better at. I think that, the thing is that he enjoyed it. You know, I think when you're good at something it's fun to do. He liked it.

Here she conceives of effective teaching as (1) adhering closely to the text, (2) having students enjoy what they read, (3) fashioning discussions that draw on student comments, (4) making good insights on the fly, and—most interesting—(5) finding fun in it, because "when you're good at something it's fun to do." These are powerful teaching attributes, and ones that Liz held with her throughout our time together and demonstrated in her teaching; they appear to be not only descriptions of her father's practice, but also influences on her own. This passage also shows that she views him as a "traditional teacher." The two sets of conceptions stood as one powerful model of teaching and created in Liz an initial skepticism toward the more progressivist, student-centered model of teaching her credentialing program put forth.

Most university components of her credentialing program put forth a consciously student-centered educational vision. Casals University espoused an approach to teaching that included an emphasis on cooperative learning, on students constructing their own meanings, on a rejection of both lecturing and the belief that listening is learning, on the presumption that different students (primarily because of cultural differences, not individual ones) learn in different ways, on a conviction that students are already experts in many things, and on a belief that teachers ought to be—in Deborah Meier's (1995) words—guides on the side, not sages on the stage. The secondary education department chair of Casals University told me that many faculty members feel their primary responsibility often lies not inside technical aspects of curriculum and instruction but inside social views of education—"the social issues of adolescence and learning how to live life in this stage of American history." He said:

We don't have a monopoly on one particular approach to education ... and there's really no consensus [here] on what approach works best ... [But] I think the majority [of our faculty] would lean very much in the direction of the cooperative teaching and the student-centered model. I think that they try to train our teachers by putting them experientially into those models, and I think that's valuable. I don't think you see much of the pedagogic presentation of the facts of education and "here are the rules that tend to typify how kids learn and now we'll do a midterm exam" kind of thing.

Liz's curriculum and instruction professor taught an approach to the teaching of English that rested primarily on progressivist, student-centered reading texts (e.g., James Marshall's *Classroom Discourse and Literary Response* and Milner and Milner's *Bridging English* [1998]). Liz's methods seminar leader (the only instructor she had for both semesters) strongly discouraged most so-called traditional or didactic methods of instruction, flatly announcing on the first day of class, "Teachers who lecture are not good teachers." Ironically, she said this while standing in the front of the room looking out at a horseshoe configuration of students at tables taking notes. In an interview, I later asked her what she thought of traditional teaching methods:

BRAD: In your opinion, what are some of the valuable components of this "traditional paradigm" you speak of?

INSTRUCTOR: Valuable components? I don't like it very much.

BRAD: The ones worth keeping. If there are any.

INSTRUCTOR: I don't think there's anything that I would keep. I really don't.

Liz was skeptical about cooperative learning and process approaches, even though her seminar leader favored them. Though the seminar leader told me, "The big thing now is cooperative learning. [It is] one of the elements of the emerging paradigm," Liz believed otherwise:

I don't know if the group work thing is good ... I don't think it's the best way to teach. I like to feel that the person in charge is an expert in her subject. It's kind and empowering of the expert to say, "Well, what do you think?" That makes me feel strong and intelligent, and yet, I'd rather have the benefit of her expertise on the subject.

After one October class meeting devoted primarily to the students examining their own prejudices and listening to their instructor extol virtues of cooperative learning, Liz sent me an e-mail that began like this:

> Well, what did you think? A cyanide capsule would have made my day just as effective and much less painful. I'm stuck with 5 hours of bullshit.... Do you know how many times I've uttered the phrase "motherfucker" in reference to this program? I've probably said it 6 times in the past 28 years prior to September and 200 in the past month and a half.

Liz expressed strong concern that her program's approach "throws out the baby with the bathwater"—that in its desire to support student-centered approaches, it fails to recognize any value in traditional methods of teaching. She continued: "[My professors] are not, so far in any of these classes, showing me the value of more traditional methods of teaching and what I can take from those methods." During another conversation she told me, "There seems to be this assumption that because we've been in school and were taught that [traditional] way, we know what to do, and now they're going to give us an alternative. But really, alternative to what? is the question. It's just useless teaching to me." She was frustrated that her program was not delineating specifics of the traditional approach so that she could see which particular features she might take (and how to employ them), and which ones (and why) she should reject. She was also implicitly favoring *concrete* approaches over *abstract* perspectives. Though both models offered specific methods, the fact that her program wrapped them inside theoretical perspectives and ways of knowing might have seemed less palatable than the "This-is-what-works" immediacy that commonly marks practitioner discourse and that characterized the model of her father. At least she *knew* her father's approach had worked for him. She found herself unwilling to abandon her father's model of teaching without knowing why she was abandoning it, or knowing which of the useful parts (she is sure there are useful parts) to adopt and how to employ them. Until her program would address these concerns, Liz was prepared to reject it.

Yet, when she talked and wrote about the particulars of her father's curricular and pedagogical approaches, she acknowledged that his teacher-centered methods were not wholly sufficient, either. She understood that her program's approach—being newer, ostensibly better researched, focused on the learner not the teacher, and legitimized by virtue of its university status—should be taken seriously. She believed this offered her an either/or decision: that adopting one meant rejecting the other. Liz spent much of the fall semester both distancing herself from her father's model of teaching and simultaneously accepting her father's influence, not sure what conclusions to draw. In a teaching journal Liz kept for her reading class, on September 22 she wrote the following:

> I had an argument this weekend with my father, who has been an English teacher for 35 years. He asked what kinds of things I'm learning. I explained that the teaching models we are learning are very different from the way he teaches. I told him that we're learning to privilege the student over the teacher, that teaching now is child-centered. This elicited, pretty much, the response I expected from him. "You'll learn that none of that works. That group work is nice in the text book but it's impossible in the classroom."

But, eight days later, in an interview with me, she voiced many of her father's arguments as her own:

> [I think that] the teacher ought to be an expert on his subject. And there's a reason that we have people who are experts on their subject and why an English teacher has a different educational background than a science teacher. It's not because he facilitates in a specific way; it's because he's got information, he's got training, and he's managed to synthesize things in an academic fashion that the science teacher doesn't, and vice versa. That's why he's the English teacher, and that's why I go to him for English class, instead of my homeroom teacher, who's the gym teacher.
>
> ... Another thing is, I think it's also difficult to do student-centered learning because it's an inefficient use of time. And one of the demands on a teacher is I only have *x* number of minutes, and I've got to get through all this stuff today. It's most efficient to just get the information out, and if you can get, let's say, ten units of information out in ten minutes, just by talking them through it. Those same ten minutes of information take ten times as long if you're going to have students create or discover on their own.

Liz grappled with how much weight to give her dad's opinions against those her university program espoused. She interpreted her program as championing an approach in which student meaning-making can best be encouraged by allowing students to work in groups, share their understandings with each other in discussions, and make use of a teacher who, in her words, "facilitates" and "scoots [students] around so they hit the right places." However, she strongly believed the teacher—as disciplinary expert—has an obligation to deliver content to students who learn from the teacher's knowledge. She viewed acceptance of the student-centered model a rejection of the teacher-as-expert and, therefore, a rejection of her father-as-model.

Further complicating this knowledge struggle were disapproving personal feelings toward two of her three professors. She did not like either her seminar leader or her curriculum and instruction professor, and I found that her personal, affective reactions to them combined with her professional, epistemological beliefs about their ideas.[3] This finding highlights separate but interconnected roles of power relations and emotion within the knowledge construction process, and underscores the link between personal relationships and professional learning: Liz's perceived disempowerment at the hands of one professor negatively influenced her learning, and her emotional dispositions toward them both shaped her interpretation of what they taught her.

I observed the incident that spawned the disempowerment. During a September curriculum and instruction class meeting, Liz felt attacked for defending a traditional, lecture-based teacher the group had read about the previous week. Liz raised her hand and announced that she did not think all lecturing was bad, that there was value in some of the teaching methods typically ascribed to "traditional" teachers, that this teacher was getting an unfair rap. The professor became visibly annoyed and publicly disagreed with Liz. After class, in the hallway, Liz said to me: "She scowled at me. Did you see that? I'll never bring up that again." And later that week when I interviewed Liz, she brought up the incident: "And I actually felt, I really felt like she was just, you know, yelling at me. Not yelling, but I definitely felt, like, slugged."

Two weeks later, Liz mentioned disagreeing with this professor on another point (where personal interest ends and political ideology begins within curriculum design) but told me she would not share her thoughts in class. I asked why not, and she replied, "I'm sick of it at this point. I could [sic] care less ... I wouldn't want to offend one of her [rolling her eyes upward] patron saints." As she felt personally attacked, Liz's affective disposition (defensive, slightly humiliated, powerless to disagree in class) might have encouraged her to reject the professor's teacher knowledge. She certainly spoke negatively of this professor all year. And several of the returned assignments Liz wrote for that class contain margin notes from the professor asking Liz not to be so dichotomous about the two teaching approaches, but Liz never referenced them to me, even when I asked her about the general nature of the professor's written feedback. As the professor's small handwriting was difficult to decipher, I wonder if Liz even read the comments.

About her seminar leader, Liz also expressed an antipathy that suggested a blending of professional and personal reactions. At various points, Liz told me the following:

> I just don't see her as a scholar, and I don't think she's an expert in her field.... And what she offers me about education—I haven't found much appreciation.
>
> [She] doesn't practice what she preaches. Tells us to always return student work quickly, but she still has yet to return any of the written work we handed in.... It's hard to take her seriously.
>
> You know, there's this point you've reached with someone, and it's like anything they say, there's just this sigh in your head. It's so wasteful.

The feeling appeared to be mutual. The instructor indicated to me in an interview, though in more qualified terms, that she felt the two of them "never really had a strong connection." She also confirmed that Liz was "not at all quick to embrace" the student-centered paradigm.

Liz liked her third instructor and found the teaching ideas solid and usable. And this raises a third teaching model: teacher-as-technician. This instructor taught a reading course, and put forward a model of effective teaching as applying researched reading techniques to multilingual classes, so fledgling English readers can use prior knowledge (or schema) to decode texts and become more literate. Her curriculum stressed direct implementation of preset exercises and activities; there was little room for a teacher's personal dimensions to enter into the teaching; and the actual teaching of this instructor reflected her stated approach, as she delivered content efficiently and quickly and handed out stacks of ready-to-use worksheets and activities. Liz found these activities useful and appreciated the no-nonsense way this instructor taught. During the second year, whenever I asked her what value she saw her program as having for her, she referenced only this instructor. Several reasons exist for why Liz unproblematically accepted this teacher's knowledge.

One is that this instructor treated Liz in ways she appreciated, even writing Liz a strong recommendation letter near the end of the semester and praising her class comments and written work. A second reason is that, as an unconfident beginner, Liz felt comforted to receive concrete methods and handouts she could directly apply in a classroom. This approach was tangible (and supported by her prior familiarity with teachers who hand out worksheets). A third reason is that this teaching model did not directly contradict her father's model of teaching: The course content could be applied in a teacher-centered classroom (even if the instructor did not intend it, as I do not think she did); accepting the teaching approach did not, for Liz, require a theoretical rejection of didactic instruction. A fourth reason is that Liz respected the professor professionally, describing her to me as a "scholar": She wrote published articles, attended academic conferences, used a specialized lexicon, and appeared to Liz more "professional" in her delivery. This instructor used little humor or levity, and the disliked seminar leader—who employed both in abundance—told me Liz suffers from a "negative moodiness ... I don't know whether she doesn't have much of a sense of humor, or whether because of her life experiences she finds it very difficult to be light." This personal incompatibility between them probably affected Liz's professional learning. And the fifth reason is that this instructor actually worked with high school students in public schools. Liz frequently raised issues of legitimacy or "street credibility" when comparing practicing teachers to university professors, once saying, "I'm sure that teachers that have actually been teaching for a number of years bring more to the discussion of traditional versus student-centered than [my program peers and instructors] do." She was pleased that her reading instructor "invented" and still teaches a classroom-based, multidistrict reading program for English-language learners.

Part Two: Grappling with Contradictions

Three months into her teacher education program, Liz felt that she could not retain both her father's model of teaching and her program's; something would have to be sacrificed. She was unwilling to abandon the notion of teacher-as-expert, believing that to do so would necessarily mean that only the students were experts and this, she believed, meant students would only learn each other's naive-learner opinions. She felt her father was right about this. Also, she agreed with her dad that group work was a cumbersome, inefficient approach that often devolved into students chatting. Yet, she knew there were tragic sacrifices inherent in the traditional approach. Analyzing the data, it appears that Liz's understanding of these sacrifices derived primarily from a second set of knowledge influences and models for teaching: her girlfriend, some memories of her own school experiences, her favorite tenth grade teacher, and her political/moral reasons for teaching. These influences deepened the process of Liz's teacher knowledge construction, because recognition of them encouraged her to reevaluate her father's teaching, clarified her interpretation of her program's model, and provided additional teaching models to consider.

Liz described a running conversation she was having with her girlfriend who encouraged her to think about who loses in a teacher-as-didactic-expert approach like her father's:

BRAD: Who do you currently talk teaching with?

LIZ: I talk to my girlfriend a bit about it. Partly because I know how much she hated school as a kid. She's just like, "I don't buy that. Please." ... For her, school was a really big problem, and it's really important for me to see that and to hear that. Partly, it's just like, okay, when that kid comes in late after lunch every day and passes notes, don't yell at her. I know how much her insecurities about her language ability and her grammar and her ability to communicate and be articulate were just like a cloud over her. I don't know what happened, but for some reason that wasn't good. So, I definitely have that in mind, to keep an eye on that. I think understanding that has really made me less of an elitist, to see that and to respect someone who's like that. And I think I'll bring that into the classroom in a way that I don't think I would have a year ago.

This reveals that because of her girlfriend's school experience, Liz came by an understanding that, as a teacher, she must never make a student insecure over his or her language difficulties. What Liz describes as a "cloud over her" Stephen Krashen (1987) would call the affective filter, but no matter the terminology, Liz believed that to engage in this emotional bullying constitutes a kind of "elitism." She accepted that a student's levels of anxiety and self-esteem relate to motivation and therefore affect learning. This notion appears to have earned its power in Liz from her personal relationship.

Liz began reevaluating her father's teaching within a similar vein:

It's interesting finding out now and taking classes now and seeing the new age of teaching and comparing it to the way I know my dad has taught for the last forty-five years and getting real disillusioned with my dad as a teacher.

BRAD: Why?

LIZ: I've seen his lesson plans. I've seen the essays and grades, and I know what he looks for. And it's like a reality check. I guess in some ways I'm finding out my dad wasn't the greatest teacher. Actually what my dad is really good at is teaching the smart class and teaching the AP classes and teaching the kids who are already there, and adding to what they know and giving them technical skills and fine-tuning them. I think the kids who need it fall to the back of the room, and that's a way that my dad is not a great teacher. My brother who's in his early thirties now has friends who are his own age who were my dad's students. And one who is smart and bright [and liked my dad as a teacher]. And another, or the sister of another is like, "Oh, your dad's Mr. Mason? He made me feel like I was nothing." She became an expert in repairing airplanes and writes manuals on how to repair airplanes. But my dad made her feel like she couldn't do anything. So that's why I want to teach.

Liz also decided that part of her father's success derives from a confidence that she does not yet possess:

I feel like if I were to do what he did, it would not work. I couldn't pull it off. I don't feel I have the sense of authority, either about the text, and authority in the sense of ownership. I sort of have to invent my sense of confidence, which is okay, because eventually it won't be invented. But he is confident in what he does and who he is, and he owns the room when he walks in. Just owns it. And that means he has less behavior problems.

These two passages reveal that as she reflected on her father's professional influence on her, she began to contextualize his success, qualify his teaching, and tease out discrete sources of his approach. Automatically, as she was evaluating him, she was choosing which components of his model to adopt, which to reject, and which would emerge over time. She was realizing that, even though his example is admirable, she did not believe she could—or would want to—be the teacher he was. The passage also communicates other features of Liz's knowledge. First, it reveals that she feels she must (and can) "sort of invent" a confidence she believes teaching requires; this is a point she made several times to me, and interestingly one that suggests Liz believes a teacher can "fake it" for a while until experience-based wisdom emerges, and one that demonstrates she believes teaching presupposes confidence: "In most respects, performance is based on confidence ... it doesn't matter if you're good or not. If you inspire trust and respect because it's something you think you're good at, then that will be enough to stand on." Second, when Liz mentions her father "owning" the room when entering it, she reveals another tacit component of her interpretation of the teacher-centered approach: an instructor who takes over a classroom, whose (teacher-centered) presence is large enough to command attention. Third, the passage uncovers that here Liz views "authority" as synonymous with "confidence" and sees a direct correlation between a teacher's confidence and the frequency of behavior problems in the classroom: Confidence leads to an authoritative presence, which decreases discipline difficulties.

She also reconsidered her own secondary school experiences. She remembered her schooling as primarily a traditional learning experience:

> In my experiences with school, group work, the kind of collaborative learning or student-centered thing, was never big. It was, "You sit here," and for fifty minutes we would do stuff. And either you write stuff or you read stuff or the teacher tells you stuff and you write it down. And that's not what school is anymore. And in part I'm glad it's not that anymore, but in part it makes it much more difficult on the teacher.

Memories of her teenage self judging teachers from the back of the classroom still held sway for her as she prepared to become a teacher: "I really believe in the '[teacher-as] expert-in-her-subject' kind of thing. I remember believing it when I was in high school. I remember feeling that the way I judged teachers was whether or not I felt they knew their subject."

Academically Liz did relatively well in junior high and high school English. She attributed this success to her English-teacher parents:

> I was a lazy student. My parents were English teachers, so somehow I got by on just having a well-trained ear. I knew, for the most part, what sounded right. I was in the smart class all through junior high school ... I cheated a bit. I discovered that if I asked my parents general questions about [Shakespeare plays, for example], I'd leave the dinner table with specific answers, interpretations, and insights. All I had to do was remember them long enough to repeat them in class the next day.

It appears, however, that, though Liz believed she got by academically, she believed she was neither learning nor happy. In a course paper dated October 27, Liz related her memories of learning vocabulary:

> I've never felt I was taught vocabulary in any meaningful way in high school ... I think that if I had had thorough, fun, and satisfying experiences with vocabulary words in high school, I might have had more facility and comfort with speaking, reading and writing than I had during and after high school.

Five times (twice in conversation with me, three times in writing assignments for her program) she recounted a story of hating school, of neither fitting in nor feeling her ideas were validated until she came across her tenth grade English teacher, who, she says, caused a turnaround. Her history raises two important features. One is that Liz can remember feeling disenfranchised by the school community she was a part of—that it (and the traditional teaching that characterized it) made her feel unwanted and unfulfilled. The second feature is that Liz credits one particular teacher with turning things around for her. In a class journal on September 8, Liz describes having had, in school, "the unbelievable feeling that I didn't fit ... never felt that I had the right clothes or cared about the right music ... the social standards of cool were beyond me ... my laziness prohibited my excelling." And then, directly following, she writes of having

> this English teacher who encouraged my insights and my writing. I read entire books for the first time. I wrote papers which, at least at the time, were well-written and thought out.... The teacher invited me to take her honors course the following year.... A friend and I became editors of the annual literary magazine [which this teacher sponsored]. It was the first time, in any academic environment, that I'd felt powerful and confident about a subject and about myself.

In another written piece for a different class, she wrote on September 14:

> I never completed a book until I was a sophomore in high school. Finally, I had an English teacher who was fun and funny. For her, I wanted to read. Thinking back, I probably just had a crush on her and wanted to prove my intellectual worth. But at least I read. For the first time, reading

didn't feel like a chore. I had insights of my own to share in class. From that year on, I was a reader. I became an Honors English student. I read novels for school and for fun.

A week later, as we were talking about why she wanted to be a teacher, I heard a similar version. After first referencing her dad, she began to talk about her own high school experiences:

> I didn't like school when I was a kid. And that's unfortunate.... But during my sophomore year I had this teacher who was the hippest, jeans-wearing English teacher. She was tough and funny and inspired insight and expression in everyone that I didn't feel I got from other teachers. It was American literature and we read *The Scarlet Letter* and *The Crucible,* and I was very happy and talked and got interested.

> BRAD: What did she do that made the environment such that this occurred?

> LIZ: I think I just had a crush on her. She was funny.... It was a lot about the thing a teacher does when they're waiting to say the thing they're thinking: "Okay. Good. And let's see if somebody else can come up with the right answer. Good Jimmy."... And her interpretations of things. She may have had a right answer in her head, but she wasn't overbearing about it.... She made me feel smart.

These passages reveal several significant points. They present another set of examples—as when she explained why her dad is a good teacher— where Liz views effective teaching as conducting discussions in which students' ideas are made to appear significant and artfully weaving together student comments and teacher expertise. During my two years of following Liz, this pedagogical facet remained an important criterion on which she evaluated herself. Describing her own teaching, she often rated herself solely on her ability to challenge and validate student comments; observing her teach, I found that teacher-led discussions composed the core of most lessons. As she described good teaching, Liz often privileged front-stage classroom pedagogy over backstage planning, assessment, and reflection. This echoes Dan Lortie's (1975) and Deborah Britzman's (1986) claims that many beginning teachers know only the visible, classroom-based aspects of teaching and underconsider curriculum design, teacher reflection, and learning assessment. This suggests that, because much of what Liz knows about teaching derives from her apprenticeship of observation, she tended to highlight what a teacher "does when they're waiting to say the thing they're thinking," or how a teacher "made me feel."

There is also the fact that she clearly (the story almost reaches Creation Myth status) considers this teacher and this semester a pivotal point not only in her schooling trajectory but also in her decision to teach. Liz remembers feeling alienated until her tenth grade English teacher brought her into the discourse/culture of classroom success by validating her ideas. This teaching model—teacher as hip, jeans-wearing, fun person who makes students feel their contributions are valued—emerged from Liz's personal history with school, and could be linked to her nascent sexuality. Additionally it appears that, again, Liz's personal feelings for a teacher became inextricably entangled with the professional model the teacher became—this time the mirror image of her relationship with both program instructors. (And it might not be coincidental that Liz often wore denim pants when teaching, even though her seminar leader/teaching supervisor discouraged it.)

And finally, several conceptions of teaching emerge from a look at Liz's language use in that first written excerpt. When in that passage she wrote, "For her, I wanted to read. Thinking back, I probably just had a crush on her and wanted to prove my intellectual worth. But at least I read," she reveals a complex feature of her knowledge. She reveals that the motivation to read came from her feelings for the teacher—that the work was carried out to impress (or "prove my intellectual worth" to) her. That Liz viewed it as acceptable ("but at least I read")—though not preferred (notice the marker "but")—for a teacher to use her relationship with students as a way to motivate them to work is a notion I found frequently when observing Liz's own teaching; it seems likely to have emerged from this tenth grade relationship. The link between her personal feelings for the teacher and her motivation to work shaped Liz's conception of an ideal teacher. Several places in interview data and observation notes disclose evidence of Liz believing that a teacher who is liked by students has an additional motivational tool at her disposal. In fact, in a later interview, I asked her what qualities she felt a successful English teacher needed to possess, and she began describing qualities she used months before to describe her tenth grade teacher. I asked, "So, is it fair to say you want to be your own tenth grade English teacher?" She agreed, adding, "I want to be the cool teacher. I want to be the person [students] come to." And, finally, memories of this experience offer a model of successful teacher as hip friend who attends to students' needs to have their ideas validated in class—a counterbalance, in some ways, to what she found disappointing in her father.

Liz's moral/political concerns for students and her reasons for teaching also shaped her views about the teacher-centered versus student-centered debate. As she recognized who was abandoned in her father's classroom and what kind of student population she hoped to teach, she concluded that her dad's model was not the best one for her intended classrooms. She believed her dad successfully taught motivated, academically comfortable students who came from predominantly white, middle-class families. Liz intended to teach a different student population. She had told me that, after she dropped out of a selective liberal arts college and enrolled in a Staten Island community college, it was her fellow students who indirectly inspired her career decision:

> I was so surprised by how inarticulate my classmates were. Not interested in reading anything. A lot of people were working part or full time and, you know, trying to get it done. That was impressive. Why do I want to teach? Clearly, I saw that there was a need. People were not getting educated in high school. The population that I've become interested in is the at-risk, whatever that means. The kids who need to know how to write a cover letter or a resume, because if they don't, they're just going to do bad things. The people who are not taken seriously because they can't communicate seriously.... And while we're so concerned with social inequality and economic reality and crime and all the complaints that conservatives seem to have, it seems ironic to deny them the best education they can have. It's a political act.

In a later interview, she again referenced this history and its influence on her career decision:

> So, I was taking this [community college] English class and I was, you know, like the smartest person in the room. And it wasn't that it was anything insightful, because it was a relatively easy class, but there was no thought process going on in that room. And that's when it occurred to me that it might be a good direction to go in.
>
> BRAD: You mean teaching?
>
> LIZ: To teach, yeah. Because [students unprepared to think deeply in college] is a real problem, and so that's when I thought to do it.

The first passage reveals an interest in teaching for social change: The sympathetic reference to students working while "trying to get it done" illuminates a socioeconomic sympathy; the quick jump from the local (her fellow students) to the universal (the at-risk population, "the kids who …") reveals that she is mapping her experience with the community college students onto her conceptual understanding of those future students she intends to teach; and the reference to "social inequality and economic reality and crime and all the complaints that conservatives seem to have" illustrates a left-leaning, sociopolitical mission underneath her reasons for teaching. The second passage echoes this, especially knowing that Liz typically minimizes her own intelligence: She is not claiming to be uniquely intelligent but, instead, is sadly surprised to be "the smartest person in the room." Her dad's teaching might be primarily a professional or academic endeavor, but she considers hers a political act.

Liz often revealed a moral obligation to give disadvantaged students access to quality schooling, frequently telling me that from her family she had learned that teaching is "this noble thing to do." In one interview she told me that

> [public school] teaching is a form of social action. If one wanted to teach students bound for success all the time, one would teach in a private school where the students are selected for their ability. If one teaches in a public school, one is therefore admitting that part of his motivation for teaching is to teach those who—is to teach everyone.

In another conversation, she told me:

> The draw for me [the attraction of being a teacher] is wanting to, I don't know how to put it, wanting to cure society. I mean, how are we being fair if we're not providing that? If we're making the best schools the ones in the expensive neighborhoods? Those kids are going to be okay anyway. Those aren't the kids that need the better schools … I want to work at a downtown school. That's the population that needs the most attention and needs the most exciting teachers.

At another point, Liz said to me, "Of course teaching is a form of social action. What else is it?" Her seminar leader/teacher supervisor confirmed this social justice undercurrent of Liz's teaching, although she cast it unfavorably, telling me, "She wants the kids to be successful. I think one of the things that I see in her, though, is that she's almost a missionary. Caught up in the cultural deficit model, and that's why she's a missionary. That can be deadly."

Employing the model of the teacher-as-agent-of-social-change did not offer Liz a way out of the student-centered versus teacher-centered teaching puzzle; in fact, it deepened the dilemma. Applying a social justice perspective to education, she admired the traditional model's strict insistence on students learning product, on students internalizing an expert teacher's content knowledge in order to eventually become competent thinkers and communicators on their own:

> I think it's important for a kid to learn what a flat character is and what a round character is, and what the setting and tone and theme and thesis and topic sentence are. Not because they're going to be asked about it later, but because those are valuable methods of analysis, valuable sign posts. And we shouldn't deny that. There's a reason a cliché is a cliché. There's a reason there are rules to grammar. And I don't think we should forget that, or say that it isn't true.

She saw a political importance to ensuring that historically underserved students learned those skills and content that she believed allowed them inside the arena of middle-class success. In several interview passages, she acknowledged that Standard English might be a culturally loaded language, but mastery of it is necessary for anyone desiring power:

> [Standard English] is not value free. I mean, maybe it's elitist in its construct or who gets to create it and who gets to decide what is and is not acceptable. Fine. It is. But that's not the issue I need to deal with now. The issue I need to deal with is how I can give students the most power. And power comes from them knowing the language of those who hold the power.

She felt strongly that previously disenfranchised students (whom she defined primarily as either recent immigrants and English-language learners or children of working-class parents) needed access to the rules and codes of English-language use if they were going to succeed in middle-class United States. She appreciated Lisa Delpit's (1995) *Other People's Children*, because her interpretation of the text allowed her to reconcile high product standards and teacher-as-expert features of her father's model with her strong desire not to disappoint those students for whom school success does not come easy. As I quoted more extensively in the previous chapter, Liz discussed this:

> [Delpit] did this great thing in the beginning of [Delpit's essay "The Silenced Dialogue"], which was something like—ah, I found out that a child can learn from being constantly corrected, and not end up fucked-up, or something like that.

In a written response to a reading assignment from Delpit's "The Politics of Teaching Literate Discourse," Liz stridently wrote:

> When I first read the Delpit article on teaching skills in a formal classroom versus teaching expression in an open classroom setting, I thought Delpit was the voice of reason. I thought that she was the first person to finally expose the disparity and unfairness of teaching students to use whole language to express the subtlest of thoughts, when what the students needed was to learn how to spell.... As educators, we need to teach grammar and writing and spelling especially to those kids who did not grow up using the codes of "white" or "traditional" education and Standard English.

It concerned her that the student-centered model she interpreted her two professors as articulating lowered expectations in the service of keeping students' affective filters down:

> We're waiting for kids to feel comfortable with learning, and in the meantime they don't know the difference between a subject and a verb and can't construct a sentence, which means they can't communicate outside the classroom. I think it's very important for kids to understand that proper English is the standard code, and is valuable.

Yet, she feared that traditional, didactic teaching, in its rigidity and emphasis on product and positivistic knowledge, precluded many students (especially those in her future) from feeling comfortable with learning: a kind of student alienation at the hands of traditional teachers. Like her girlfriend who was made to feel insecure about the things she did not know, or the student who found Liz's father demoralizing, Liz appreciated an interpretation of student-centered teaching that accepted that a student's emotional comfort correlates to learning:

> When a mind is developing, it's important to give the person the opportunity to explore and feel free and "safe"—that's the word of the day—to

do that. To sort of develop and to think and to have opinions and ideas and change his mind and to interpret in his own twisted way or his correct way. That's the really incredible, valuable thing of student-centered or group or collaborative learning.[4]

Liz was also afraid that traditional approaches, in their insistence on standardization, did not fit all kinds of learners. She told me, "For all the things with which I disagree in Casals University's credential program, the things with which I do agree are the responsibility of the teacher to vary his or her methods to meet needs and to recognize the needs and capabilities of different students." It seems here that she values the goals of Casals but not the means. Liz wants to adopt a version of the student-centered model of teaching. She finds its egalitarian contours aligned with her political reasons for teaching. She believes its emphasis on activity better captures student attention ("because I think that there's more student activity [in the student-centered model], and I think activity prevents boredom and I think boredom is the devil in teaching"). Yet, four primary obstacles seem to prevent her adopting it: One is that she believes she does not know how to do it, as opposed to the teacher-centered model she believes she knows intimately (from her apprenticeship of observation and her father); the second is that she believes it has the tendency to dilute learning in favor of student safety; the third is that she finds it an inefficient use of time and materials; and the fourth is that her respect for practice-based educators (her dad and the mostly traditional teachers she observed and talked with) and disrespect for theory-based educators (her two primary professors) give rise to a skepticism of the—still abstract to her—conceptions of cooperative/student-centered instruction. Such is the complex disposition with which Liz entered her student teaching.

Part Three: Liz Teaches

The Beginning. Liz carried out her student teaching practicum from January until June 2000 at a midsized, comprehensive public high school in a small, diverse city thirty miles from her home. I call it Montenegro High School. Montenegro High enrolls 1,700 students in grades nine through twelve and categorizes itself as an "urban fringe" school. In 2000, self-report data designated 36 percent of its students as limited-English proficient (or LEP) and 24 percent as qualifying for free or reduced lunches. Latino and Caucasian populations constitute more than half of the student body, with Asian and African-American populations second and third, respectively (Education Data Partnership 2000). Her university practicum requirements obligated her to teach two English classes each day until the school year ended in June; she would typically have had a cooperating or "master" teacher for each class, but, because she applied for and was accepted to receive payment for one of the classes she taught (the school was understaffed that year), it was designated an "internship," and she had no master teacher for that course. She was therefore an intern teacher for one class (tenth grade English as a second language) and a student teacher for the other (ninth grade English). Because Montenegro employed a block schedule, Liz taught two ninety-minute periods five days each week. Liz chose this school from among five options, even though it entailed an almost three-hour bus commute each day, because she liked the school and because she wanted to earn money teaching, and she chose the one master teacher/class with which she participated because, she said simply, she liked the teacher's "style." In June, she was offered a full-time position, which she accepted, and therefore taught English there the next year, too.

In January 1999, weeks before beginning her student teaching, Liz was required to write a "Classroom Management Plan" for her university seminar, which articulated her teaching philosophy and identified features of her ideal classroom environment and her discipline rules. Analysis of this document reveals that Liz continued to favor personal knowledge sources over programmatic ones and expected to blend together teacher-centered and student-centered instructional features into a hybrid she believed would combine the best from each approach while avoiding the problems of each.

The first three sentences of this document foreground her apprenticeship of observation and emphasize a professional debt, almost destiny, to her familial upbringing:

> I don't remember a time when I didn't consider teaching. It was kind of family business in our house. As I grew up, it was always in the back of my mind, a future thing, like having children and a home, something to which I looked forward but didn't know I'd grow into.

Next, she subtly suggests she always knew how to teach but simply needed some comfort and to polish her abilities: "I feel now that each step I have taken in my academic education and in my social education have been steps preparing me not only for a comfort with teaching, but steps which have helped me to hone my teaching abilities." This sentence supports the emphasis on professional comfort and confidence Liz previously established as a significant tenet for her—the only result Liz expected from her program when we first talked. It also articulates a theme that emerged often as a knowledge influence in the development of her teacher thinking: Liz believed that being an effective teacher was about being expert in one's subject, caring about students, and being a reflective hard worker who learns primarily from one's own teaching experiences. This predisposed her not to expect much from her program and to lean heavily on personal sources like her father, the teachers she remembers having, and her own frames of reference. The sentence quoted previously furthers the idea that most of Liz's life, as she viewed it, had been preparation for teaching—not that teaching is necessarily in her nature but surely in her nurture. The finding that many beginners believe "a teacher is born not made" is common (e.g., Calderhead 1988; Weinstein 1989), yet this particular aspect of Liz's knowledge suggests a third option: someone neither born a teacher nor "made" a teacher (by a teaching program, anyway). Instead, it indicates someone who is *raised to be* a teacher. And the final clause further demonstrates Liz's belief that her teaching abilities have always been with her—needing only to be "honed" by the academic and social steps she has taken. This notion of a beginning teacher believing she has forever possessed teaching abilities while viewing a credentialing program as mere finishing school is not an uncommon conception (Calderhead 1988; Holt-Reynolds 1992; Lortie 1975; Weinstein 1989), but it is noteworthy that, one semester into her program, she continued to hold the conception. Surely, it is one her Casals instructors would reject.

In the section called "Classroom Environment," Liz reveals her blending of student-centered teaching beliefs and teacher-centered ones. She defines a classroom as a "societal microcosm," an assertion that softens the individualistic framing of a previous paragraph and tacitly invokes her program's social learning focus. Liz then writes, "As a teacher I will use the authority I have to create an environment in which students' thoughts, concerns and ideas are just as important—frequently more important—than mine." This implicit nod to her own tenth grade teacher's success joins Liz's own past to the student-centered focus of Casals. This link importantly demonstrates that those features of her credentialing program aligned with positive aspects of her biography stand a better chance of acceptance into her teacher knowledge; because she valued her own teacher legitimizing her student ideas, she is disposed to accept those parts of her program that seek the same for her students. She then writes that she favors a horseshoe pattern arrangement of desks over a circle, because every student should be able to see the teacher and the board—a teacher-centered detail her father espoused (and her program modeled, even while she articulated otherwise). However, three weeks into her teaching, Liz moved the desks into rows, because "It didn't work. It was just constant talking everywhere.... They could see everybody." A seating structure where "students could see everybody" was a feature her program would applaud, but Liz found that it created a chaos she could not accept. She retained the row structure through the second year, too.

In the concluding section, Liz returns to personal, historical domains to locate her teaching models, conspicuously favoring the influence of past teachers and her own high school experiences over any university sources of teacher knowledge, and putting her ultimate faith for teacher success in nonspecialized human traits like respect and subject passion:

> As a high school student myself, I found that the difference between a class in which I misbehaved, cut or just didn't put much effort, and one in which I excelled, was the degree to which I felt that the teacher respected me. These teachers are the ones I remember, the ones I found inspirational not only because of their passion for their subjects, but also because it was important to them that I find a meaning and passion of my own in the subjects as well.... I hope to be such a teacher.

Liz references her teachers' respect for students, a teacher's passion for the subject (and ability to instill that passion in students), and teachers privileging student voices in order to allow a kind of student ownership that motivates further learning. These are features her program would recommend and, in fact, advocated, yet Liz credits only her own student experiences and her own teacher models as their source. She does not cite any of the texts, theorists, or instructors from her program (even knowing, surely, that credit to her seminar leader—the target audience of this paper—would likely hold her in good stead). She does not mention coursework or employ any of the jargon her program used ("cooperative," "student-centered," "paradigm," "learning strategies," "cultural sensitivity," "anti-racist," "multicultural"). Instead, she references her personal history and puts her faith in those fundamentally human features she believes constitute successful teaching.

The Teaching as Influence

Liz's actual teaching experience generated a new—and very immediate—source of professional knowledge. Rather than introduce new models for teaching, the data reveal that this three-semester experience both altered and reinforced existing models with which she had been grappling. Most significantly, Liz lowered her social and academic expectations of her students and, in doing so, shifted the locus of agency off her students (and therefore off herself) and onto society. She also distanced herself-as-student from the lives of her students, believing that their experiences dramatically differed from her own (a recognition that led her to abandon the teacher-as-friend model). Additionally, I found that her ambivalence toward the student-centered model and teacher-centered model of teaching, and the resulting patchwork hybrid she fashioned, was strengthened—but not modified much—by her experience teaching: She continued to grapple with both sides and still struggled with a way to combine them successfully.

The story of "reality shock" in teaching—beginning teacher confronts a classroom reality more difficult than anticipated and, in the face of it, lowers expectations and abandons previously held beliefs about teaching and students—is an oft-told tale (Rust 1994; Veenman 1984). Unsurprisingly, I found it occurred for Liz. But rather than tell it here, I have chosen to focus on how Liz's beginning teaching experience influenced the narrative this chapter has deigned to present thus far. Teaching caused her to recast her relationship with students, abandon the teacher-as-friend model, and slightly reassemble her relationships to her father's model and that of her credentialing program.

She found teaching more difficult than she predicted, and her conceptions of student agency changed. After teaching only a few weeks, Liz began to believe that her students were not motivated to work hard simply because their new teacher validated their thoughts, respected them, knew the material, and held high expectations for their success. She felt frustrated that students respected neither the behavioral norms nor the academic lessons she put forth; she felt that they took advantage of her (student-centered) attention on their success:

A lot of those kids ... feel that the fact that they are [even in class] is something for which the teacher should be thankful.... And that they should be able to eat whenever they want and should be able to get up and talk to somebody else across the room whenever they want. I think that [their previous teacher] was a lot more lenient with them than I am. But I can't teach that way. Maybe she can.

Liz had first believed strongly in individual student agency, telling me in November, "the responsibility to perform always relies on the student, always falls on the student," but she began to soften this conception. At the end of January, she said, "the motivating factor for a student's ability or inability to perform may certainly fall outside his control. I'm taking into consideration where he's coming from, but certainly he's the one that has to perform." Soon, Liz began positing more and more factors affecting student success that she believed lay outside students' control, often contrasting her home culture against theirs:

I know that for me, you know, my parents made sure I was in line, that I did the work I needed to do. They'd find out if I wasn't doing my homework. I'd get yelled at. I don't know that that's the kind of guidance that all these kids are getting when 60 percent of that school is an immigrant population. I certainly think that poor immigrant families have a lot more on their minds to deal with, with their families, than sitting over their kids' shoulders to make sure they're doing their homework.

The passage again demonstrates that Liz typically views teaching and her students through her own personal experience, though it suggests she has begun differentiating between her and their experiences. As she became familiar with her students, she believed that because their backgrounds were different, she was less able to connect with them.

Also, as she accounted for differences between her (or, more accurately, her memories of herself as a high school student) and these students, she subtly constructed *their* identities using *her* notions of immigrants, their family influences, and their status as financially poor. As she did this, it seems that she unknowingly invited in a host of cultural assumptions and generalizations about the academic motivation and capacities of poor immigrant students of color. Her unawareness of this process and of the information she used to construct understandings of students brings us into the realm of middle-class white teachers teaching working-class students of color and falling victim to bias, oppression, and cultural construction. She found the quality of students' skills—writing, speaking, homework, intellectual analysis—disappointingly low. To explain this vast distance between their skills and those she expected, she located their failings inside societal disenfranchisement, poverty, and immigration. She placed blame on their families but only indirectly, because she also viewed the families as victims of larger dimensions of discrimination and disadvantage. Students' low skills and motivation were not their fault, she reasoned, and not her fault, but rather the fault of the system. Liz found herself grappling with her expectations of students. Comments in February capture this ambivalence:

> BRAD: What do you think about [your master teacher calling your expectations too high]?
>
> LIZ: I find it offensive. I think any kid can—I don't like that excuse, but I get it from kids, too. It's just the way I act. I've always been this way. [Students ask me,] "What do you expect from me?" Well, "I expect you to grow up ... to behave like an adult, to work as hard as you can." It's weird because a lot of those kids seem really sad. Like they feel they've already been defeated by the school or society or something. I'm starting to think about that.

She views herself as expecting the best from people, a disposition she believes derives from her personality ("just the way I act"). She appears surprised that this disposition is unusual, believing that anything less is "offensive" (appearing to invoke, in its moral undertones, the teacher-as-social-change-agent). But she has also begun facing the possibility that her expectations are misaligned with reality: that an unfair but very real pressure exerts itself in a way that cripples these students' ability to carry out their school obligations.[5] This ambivalence remained during the two years as she searched for a balance that suited her.[6] Observing her teach, I identified countless places where her particular view of student efficacy—a fragile mix of student agency and student powerlessness—emerged in the classroom. Some days she treated students as if they had significant agency over their actions and learning: She would tell them (and me) that the onus of succeeding in school, and in life, "fell on" each of them. Other days she would attribute student failure to a lack of support from family, from the school culture, from society—conceiving of students as products of larger forces. Interestingly, she always attributed their *successes* solely to themselves ("He's just so smart." "She works hard." "Because he's more mature than the others."). It appears that her compassion for her students created an inherent reluctance to blame them for failure yet an instant willingness to credit them for success—a perhaps logical incongruence existing as a kind of emotional equilibrium. She was searching for justifications of her own practice, and doing that necessitated a fragile, almost illogical, mix of individual agency and structural determinism. She began the semester claiming that any lack of student success was probably her fault, because she was inexperienced. But after a while she began, almost protectively, defending her teaching and, instead, pointed to social forces that precluded her students' success. By the following year, Liz had begun articulating whole litanies of variables outside her—and her students'—control that she believed negatively affected her teaching and their learning.

After teaching multiple units on vocabulary, parts of speech, pronoun usage, and compound and complex sentences, Liz reevaluated her beliefs about teaching grammar. Once so fundamental to her social mission ("mastery of English equals power"), so central to her conceptions of English ("Do you have any grammar stuff?"), and so reminiscent of her own upbringing ("I grew up being corrected, listening to my English teacher parents talk"), her ardor toward standard language use and the prominence it received in her curriculum cooled:

> I didn't know this going in, but a grammar book is really a guide, a reinforcement, not something to necessarily teach all the way through. Going in I was trying to get through every page of this damn book. Now I know that the nuances of the present perfect continuous are not what's as important as, when you want to say something that started in the past and is still going—what do you do? Expression is more important.

Or in another interview:

> Grammar is not as important to me now. I think that I am seeing that what somebody has to express is of greater value. One should learn to [communicate] in the most effective manner and perhaps it's a detriment that I've been around kids with such poor grammatical skills that I'm able now to translate and interpret what they mean. I guess I'm widening the berth of what I will allow.
>
> BRAD: What's caused this shift in you?
>
> LIZ: I think in some ways it's seeing the skills that kids are coming in with, and they're not particularly good.... [Now] I will not judge people. Because of the kids I've had, I'm becoming a much less judgmental person.

As we continued talking, Liz moved this conversation into one that shifted agency off individual students (and herself) and onto the schools and society in which the students exist: "When we're judging [students' language use] we're judging our own ability or inability to educate. It's unfair, it's discriminatory to judge a fourteen-year-old, because what we're really judging is the quality of the educational system from which he or she came. It's the school or the culture's fault." She told me it no longer bothers her that her girlfriend pronounces "especially" as "ex-specially," nor does it "grate on" her when students mispronounce words, neglect to use "whom," or, every now and then, substitute Spanish for English. By May, she was typically talking like this: "I still believe there are certain things kids should get. But I also think that there are certain things—I don't know, I just hope that in any class I teach kids will at least end up better than they started. I hope that's true [here]."

Watching and talking with Liz during her second year at Montenegro, it was clear her expectations were substantially lower than when she began. She now allowed students to choose not to read aloud if they wished; at the end of silent, sustained reading, she no longer asked students to describe their books to the class. I asked her if she knew that, during silent, sustained reading, the boy next to me looked at the back cover of an atlas for twenty minutes:

> Yeah, I don't care.... It doesn't really matter to me what they're reading as long as there's something that they're looking at. I don't care what they read. [One student] has been looking at a legal writing book for, like, a week or two weeks. She says she wants to be a lawyer. You know, I don't know if she understands it or not. Probably not. But there's something she's drawn to in it. So I'm fine with that.... But even if it's just looking at the pictures, I think that's reading, that's interpretation. That's in some way text.

Exiting Disposition

On May 9 and 10, 2000, I shadowed Liz for two full days at Montenegro High. After the second day, she and I talked for two tape-recorded hours in her classroom. This final snapshot of her teaching and talking about teaching revealed that in some ways Liz's initial views about teaching had changed, and in other ways they had deepened. Both aspects appeared to cause her anguish. I have structured this concluding discussion around prior themes to demonstrate the ways her teacher knowledge was recursively developed.

Her ideas about her father's teaching model had developed but did not dramatically change. She concluded that her dad was a good teacher, but with two important provisos that allowed her to retain pieces of his model while simultaneously rejecting its philosophical core. One, she decided that he was an effective teacher only for "higher end," older students—those who worked hard, succeeded often, and could learn from a teacher who, primarily, talked about literature and writing and challenged students to think hard and write well. She concluded that these students could more or less teach themselves, needing her father primarily as someone who provided interesting insights and an intellectual environment. She decided that his mostly advanced placement students were very different from hers: "[His students were okay with] this kind of very traditional, old school kind of setting ... fifty-minute periods and discussion then reading then lecture. You know, your basic stuff.... [But] I couldn't pull it off." Yet, she also believed that there were components of her dad's traditional model that she could—and should—employ. Instead of the zero-sum, binary frame she first employed, she now fully embraced a hybridization of teacher-centered and student-centered instructional approaches. She believed she did not have to *replace* progressivist approaches with her father's traditional methods; she could *supplement* them with elements from her dad's model. Thus, she would stand at the front of the room and offer quasi-expert interpretations of the text, yet also implement student-centered activities and remain sensitive to student attitudes and interpretations.

I saw her enact a lesson on the beginning scenes of *Romeo and Juliet* that attempted this blend. She created a discursive structure that employed the external framework of a teacher monologue—teacher informs students of textual meanings, connections, and contexts—while inside it facilitating a back-and-forth student-centered conversation where she asked questions, listened to responses, and tried to weave student comments into her own mini-lecture. She took this dialogue-within-a-monologue where she wanted it to go, but attempted to use student answers and comments to arrive there. This student conversation wrapped inside a teacher lecture emerged as the linguistic structure Liz favored.

Two, she accepted that her father's model succeeded in large part because he had decades of practice: "I now think it may have been easier [for him], or looked easier, because he had been doing it for so long before

I showed up." Entering teaching, Liz had believed she was immediately ready to be an effective teacher; she had conceived of teaching—stemming from her many, often personal, sources of knowledge—as merely knowing one's subject, being thoughtful, remembering one's own past, and respecting all students. This entering disposition led her to believe she would teach well fast. However, she found the situation to be otherwise, and likewise reconceived her ideas about teaching. Now, for her, effective teaching required a deep intuition about students and proper pacing, a masterful ability to explain concepts and "make good insights on the fly," a patience that results from confidence, and "a firmer hand" with discipline. Interestingly, though, she believed these characteristics came from experience—not further or better training.

Also, she had initially believed an effective teacher must be expert in his or her subject (a belief deriving from her father's model): "Sometimes I feel like a bit of a fraud. I mean I graduated with an English degree ... but the list of books I have completed is unbelievably short. I feel like a phony—that I'll be found out one of these days." Yet, she had changed that view, now concluding that subject expertise emerges with experience, and she should not feel bad for not yet knowing her subject well. During her second year, she told me that "being competent" is enough, and she acknowledged that because of time constraints she sometimes merely skims through the reading assignment the night before. She concluded that she will learn by reflecting on and improving her own classroom practice, not by more successfully adhering to her program's knowledge.

The teaching methods her program espoused rarely appeared in her teaching or her talk about teaching. When I asked her how she planned units and lessons, rather than reference the seven-point Madeline Hunter (1982) approach her seminar leader had required, she articulated an alternative approach:

> You talk to most teachers and you say, "How do you plan?" or, "What does your lesson plan look like?" And they say it's a post-it note.... When I do unit plans I really just look at the thing—the book or the text—and try and figure out what skills I can hit with it. I guess I really think of it in terms of skills. Like, we're doing a play so we can do paraphrasing.
>
> BRAD: Why do you focus on skills?
>
> LIZ: Because I feel extremely pressured to teach skills from the state standards. Casals didn't tell me about that.... [But anyway], then I break

it into weeks, and what I'm going to get through at what time, and how long things are going to take.

BRAD: Do you follow the seven-part lesson plan that [your seminar leader] had you use last year?

LIZ: No. No, none of it.

She employed some of the concrete techniques her program espoused: writing an agenda on the board each day, putting students in pairs or small groups to work on a question or activity before whole-group discussions, and generating questions and prompts to link students' cultures to academic material. And she used worksheets from her Casals reading professor, telling me, "Her stuff is the only stuff I use." And notice that, in using the noun *stuff*, Liz privileges the concrete (strategies, handouts, specific methods) over abstract "ideas." But deeper ways of knowing, of viewing students and the teacher's relationship to them, and of what constitutes learning from Casals remained outside Liz's teacher knowledge. Unless I prompted her, Liz never once referenced her program the second year, instead invoking her own thinking or past experiences when providing sources for her teaching approaches. When I did prompt her (on three different occasions) to talk about the legacy of Casals, she cited her reading teacher and told me that she received nothing else of value from Casals. Her seminar leader told me that the seminar was framed around the California State Teaching Standards (California Commission on Teacher Credentialing 1997), which guided the curriculum, and which every student learned. Yet, when I asked Liz about the standards, she could not recall any of them. Even when she talked about cooperative learning—the hallmark of her program—she employed lay terms rather than the specialized language her instructors used. In a final e-mail to Liz, I extracted some phrases and concepts from her university coursework and asked her to write what she remembered about them; in her written reply she correctly described two (of three) from her reading course, one (of three) from her curriculum and instruction course, and for the rest she wrote: "Fuck if I can remember … it's escaped my brain. Sorry."

Stemming from her own tenth grade English experience, Liz initially valued the model of hip teacher who befriends students and validates them, and in doing so brings them into the arena of enjoying and succeeding in school. But as Liz distanced herself and her schooling experiences from her students and their experiences, she ceased to invoke this model in interviews or exhibit it in the classroom. Part of the reason seems to have been that she was sometimes nervous and insecure as a teacher and felt uncomfortable around these virtual strangers; part was that she was less familiar with adolescents than she expected (having had no prior experience with this age group); and part was that she felt unable to enter the unfamiliar cultures she believed they inhabited. Whether or not her students perceived it, Liz felt separated from them ("I don't know what their world is"). She continued to believe she had the right to be their teacher, but she no longer felt she had any right to be their friend. She offered her own version of the "cool" teacher, by putting rock-and-roll posters up in the classroom (but her tastes, not theirs) and having an acoustic guitar behind her desk for students to play before class. She still attempted to validate and legitimize student ideas whenever possible, and vacillated between a kind of formal, lower-octave "teacher speak" (usually at the beginning of class or when transitioning between lesson phases) and a less formalized, higher-pitched, vernacular "peer speak" before class began and in the middle of lesson phases. It was as if she talked *at* students at the beginning of a phase and talked *with* them once things heated up. Yet, she acted formal and self-conscious—standing back from the groups when circulating, crossing her arms in front of her when talking with students, rarely crouching down to be at eye level with sitting students or leaning toward them, only referencing students' personal worlds when addressing the whole group.

She continued to feel ambivalent about didactic teaching versus student-centered teaching, still trying to combine them both yet still frustrated by their apparent irreconcilability. She valued cooperative learning, privileging student knowledge, and a view of teacher as facilitator, because these features created student comfort in the classroom, which, in theory, both motivated learning and encouraged students to construct their own understandings. Yet, she lamented two primary aspects. One is that she found them difficult to implement:

> [Student-centered instruction] makes it much more difficult for me. I guess I feel like it's harder to be good at this kind of teaching, teaching in this kind of structure ... harder to teach in a student-centered environment. It's harder to get information across, because the audience is not passive. It's not an audience. But perhaps the student comes away with more of a kind of, you know, holistic sense of knowledge, or of learning.

She believed that teacher-centered instruction allowed for efficient content delivery, and Liz was reluctant to forgo that, still holding on to the belief that good teaching required students to internalize expert conceptions of writing, thinking, and knowing the literary canon.

And a second aspect she lamented is that she found that this kind of sensitivity to and respect for students created a chaotic climate that decreased her own classroom comfort. She talked about the fact that, in order to preserve some of her learning goals for students, she had to sacrifice others; and she spoke of a paradox where, if she demanded strict attention and a constant commitment to learning, students rebelled and became too disobedient to participate. Returning to the tape-recorded conversation that began this chapter, we can now better understand why Liz chose to accept less order and less learning in exchange for *some* order and *some* learning:

> And so I had to make a decision, which is: Am I gonna keep pulling and kicking kids out and having, you know, what could be mutiny—what's been mutiny—or do I try and relax a little bit and hope for as much as I can get? And I went for the latter, which means that less gets done and there's more chaos, but there's less mutiny.

This trade-off she constructs is revealing. From her own schooling experiences and her father as a model, she has come to believe that, for her, classroom order is required for students to have the focus necessary for learning. This teacher-centered conception supports the "drill-and-kill," didactic instructional approaches favored in many traditional classrooms. That Liz retained the traditional model's emphasis on order while simultaneously attempting a student-centered, progressivist environment where student ideas and student-centered discussion are favored meant she must confront the paradox that resulted. And that is exactly what happened. Her comfort capacity derived from her dad's model, but her education goals were decidedly those of her program; this mismatch created a troubling dissonance for her. This dissonance caused a professional dissatisfaction linked to a personal sorrow I will discuss in a moment:

> The tighter I try and hold them [students] the more angry I am. By the end of the day I'm miserable, and they're miserable. The more miserable they are, the less likely they are to return anything positive. And beyond all the stuff I want them to know, I don't want them to hate English or hate

school. I want them to find something in it that they like or something in it that they feel they have grown in. And I don't really see those changes.

Watching her teach, I observed this paradox. On one hand, she demanded a very quiet and ordered classroom, admonishing students for even whispering to each other (even when, as I overheard, the comments were on-topic cross-talk), prohibiting students to speak unless they raised their hands. Her diction was severe: "Wait a second." "You're not Daniel." "Ignore him until he raises his hand." She stood at the front of the room, often behind a lectern, facing rows of students in desks. There was the perceptible sense that their energy was being kept at bay, that they were uncomfortable with the tight rein, and that Liz was a constraining force. Yet, on the other hand, Liz would encourage whole-group discussions, eagerly inviting students to speak, trying to rephrase or expand students' comments to make them clearer and more insightful (like her own favorite teacher), and she would initiate activities for students to "partner up" and paraphrase lines from the text or discuss a question on their own terms.

And finally, her initial reasons for entry into the profession now appeared distant, and this saddened her. Unprompted, Liz compared prior influences on her teacher knowledge with her present views about teaching, and in doing so, she revealed that she continued to view her teaching through the lens of her own student experiences and that teaching was not what she had initially envisioned:

> The reasons I went into teaching were much more immediate last year than I think they are now.
>
> BRAD: What were those reasons?
>
> LIZ: Empowerment—empowering students. What good teaching meant to me as a kid, the change that that had on—the effect it had on me. What I enjoyed, the bits of school I enjoyed, and kind of wanting to offer that. Social change—social change is a big, big part of that. And I don't really feel any of that now.
>
> I'm not feeling much joy about [teaching]. I don't get up in the morning and say, "Gosh, I love my job." I generally get up Monday and say, "Fuck," or, "Okay, I get to come back [home] in x number of hours," or, you know, "Only five more of these [days] until the weekend." It's awful, just an awful feeling. It's not what I wanted to feel about it. It's not what

I wanted this to be [*sic*]. Last year it was something I wanted to do. This year, it's not.

During the first year she not only talked about empowering students, she also said she believed teaching empowered the teacher. She used her father as the gauge, linking part of his success to the fact that he liked doing it. Because her father enjoyed teaching so much, she presumed teaching was an enjoyable career. Although at least one of her Casals program instructors talked about the first few years of teaching often being difficult and frustrating, Liz used her father-as-model instead and compared his apparently constant satisfaction with her current dissatisfaction. She never, however, speculated aloud to me whether he liked teaching when he first began; she appeared to presume that the wholly satisfied teacher she knew growing up was the same teacher when he began. She acknowledged that his competence might have increased, but never discussed changes in his satisfaction, saying only, "I think he always loved teaching." Counting the years, I can hypothesize that her father had probably been teaching ten years before Liz was born. That means he had been teaching approximately twenty-three years by the time Liz entered high school.

She was finding that her teaching negatively influenced her personal life: "Teaching is like a cancer that takes over your whole life." Liz told me several times that teaching was ruining her relationship with her girlfriend. She attributed this not only to the enormity of the time spent on teaching ("It's exhausting. I don't go out at night. I work all Saturday.") but also to the emotional grief ("Even if I'm not working I'm so anxious about it … my feelings about [teaching] are causing distress in my relationship…. I think my girlfriend probably wants me to quit."). She told me it was difficult to remove her negative feelings about her job from her actual classroom interactions and lesson planning, saying that it takes a conscious effort to remain positive, especially with her two "trouble" classes. As we concluded this final interview, Liz said she looked forward to summer. She hoped to sleep, reconnect with her girlfriend, sleep more, and play music. She told me she was definitely going to teach next year and made no mention of considering an exit from the profession (to do so, I suspect, would be highly dispreferred, given family pressure and the fact that she believed most of her life had focused on her having a career teaching). She simply wanted to rest and not think about classrooms for a while.

Concluding Discussion

For analysis of Liz's experience learning to teach, it might help to use the graphical representation of the knowledge process, Figure 1.1, reprinted below.

The teacher identity development Liz constructed over two years changed, and its contents—which are, in fact, not static "contents" at all but an interdependent, dynamic bundle of beliefs, dispositions, goals, approaches, and identity facets—when she exited can be called her exiting "teacher knowledge," or, even more accurately, her teacher identity. As her case study illustrates, Liz's professional identity construction process is, in fact, something being continually structured out of various memories, social relationships, and past and present experiences and people. Liz was automatically constructing this evolving web of influences and effects as she continually attempted to meet her goals for herself and her students in education.

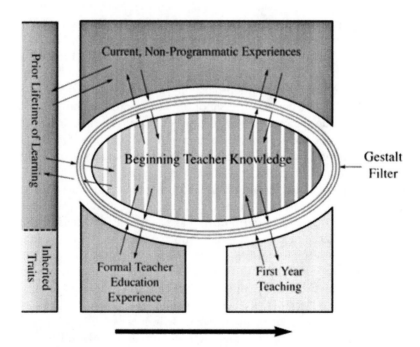

Figure 1.1   The Knowledge Process of Beginning Teacher Learning

I believe that some of this identity work was conscious and intentional and some was automatic and subconscious. Her memories of her father as teacher and her present conversations with him about teaching proved to be a powerful source of knowledge that she employed as the traditional English-teacher model. She used this model as the default lens through which to interpret her preparation program, tending to frequently conclude that Casals's cooperative, student-centered model of teaching directly opposed her dad's. Likewise, she relied on a secondary set of influences—high school memories, her girlfriend, personal feelings toward her professors—to deepen the two sides and ultimately arrive at the conclusion that, though there were good principles and practices to extract from Casals's model, she would not abandon the philosophical core of her dad's approach. In the forge of classroom teaching, she then fashioned an uneasy hybrid of the two that she believed offered a kind of coherence for her, but that ultimately did not appear to be effective for her. In fact, this hybrid was better at revealing the flaws of each side than it was in creating a beneficial blend.

I believe this ending could have been avoided. A teacher preparation program can make this holistic knowledge/identity process explicit to student teachers and therefore effect a sea change in an individual's professional learning. It can remind teacher educators that their own interpersonal relationships with students have an influence on how the students value their program's professional knowledge. It can scaffold novices like Liz into active conversation about how one's past affects the present; how one's personal identity dimensions interact with professional development; and how teacher preparation is always personalized, holistic, and continuous. Instead of the knowledge sources having power over the knower, the opposite can occur: The adult knower, in concert with others, directs the professional learning. This is a kind of metacognition widened up to holistic proportions; in the final chapter, I refer to it as "teacher identity awareness." If Liz had been more fully and consciously invited into the identity conflict(s) this chapter has illuminated, she would have become aware of the multiple identities and knowledge sources at play and the resulting identity dissonance she felt. Supported by teacher educators who understand this process, she could have reflected on what was happening and why and could have made conscious choices about which identities and knowledges to privilege and which to delimit or expel. This is how I believe beginning teachers can more actively and consciously collaborate in the construction of their own professional learning.

Notes

1. The concept of a *self* is of course problematic. Questions surrounding the narrowness of individualistic framings and potential neglect of powerful social, contextual, and historical features accompany any thoughtful discussion. I believe a "self" is, in fact, a continuous negotiation between self and other, between I and me, subject and object, between an individual and surrounding social webs (Buber 1974; Holquist 1990; Rosaldo 1989; Woods 1996). A self exists as a process as much as a product. I look to G. H. Mead (1964/1932), Holland et al. (1998), Scheibe (1995), and others for my approach: an inquiry that understands experience from the standpoint of the individual, but undertakes to determine this experience with full recognition that any individual belongs to—and is therefore shaped by—socially constructed contexts. Though this chapter focuses on Liz as an individual, I do not mean to suggest boundaries can easily be drawn.

2. I define *metaphor,* using Lakoff and Johnson (1980) and Lakoff and Turner (1989), as a conceptual schema from one domain imported into another domain that, in part, structures a person's understanding of this new domain. A metaphor organizes our knowledge by acting as a cognitive model of some previously known aspect of the world that we rely on to create understanding or communication of a new aspect.

3. I presume there is a structurally similar relationship with her father and the resulting professional influence received from him, but that personal relationship emerged in the data only to a limited degree, and I felt neither qualified nor entitled to probe her relationship with her father more deeply.

4. But notice her distancing strategy—"that's the word of the day"— which suggests she has not fully bought into the concept of safety for students.

5. I find it interesting that she does not consider the idea of resistance on the part of these students. She does not consider that, perhaps, these students are opting out because the school culture is not their culture (Kohl 1991; Ogbu 1988, 1990a, 1990b; Willis 1981). Perhaps this is because her own experiences have typically positioned her inside the various cultures of power/schooling and made it, at this point in her development, inconceivable to hold a fully antagonistic stance to this culture of power.

6. Also important is that the extent to which she posits *student* agency affects how much *teacher* agency she accepts. Each particular framing dictates how much responsibility (and therefore guilt—for she finds students' performance lamentable) she can expect to accept.

3

Life Themes
Personal Experience as Influence on Knowledge Construction— Azar, Kimberly, William, and Liz

Today is made of yesterday.

—*Anne Sexton*

The previous chapter conceptualized learning to teach as a process of assembling a professional identity out of past and present, personal and programmatic experiences. This chapter examines professional knowledge in four beginners in order to highlight individual knowledge strands and their interrelated influence on pre-service teacher identity development. The chapter is about four teacher candidates with different backgrounds and schooling experiences, different professional purposes and prior conceptions of teaching, who attended four different credentialing programs and became four different kinds of teacher. Although this may sound simple, it is not. Within their four experiences lies a complex tension between, on the one hand, the almost infinite human variation that inevitably exists and, on the other, a common set of learning patterns and epistemological principles structuring teacher identity development. By investigating the experiences of Azar, Kimberly, William, and Liz, this chapter illuminates ways in which learning-to-teach is simultaneously an individualized biographical process, a product of social constructions and contexts, and the result of generalized knowledge principles.

During analyses of the data, I found that a common knowledge/identity process occurred—one in which both a set of *reasons for entry* into the profession and a related *incoming disposition* about teaching, learning, and schooling were created through prior negotiation among a defined set of lived experiences (home/family, elementary schooling, secondary schooling, college, prior work with kids, personal relationships) inside an identifiable social *episteme* (cultural positionings and the contemporary knowledge climate). During the credentialing experience and first-year teaching this incoming disposition (with its constituent understandings, roles, and goals) was continuously being reconsidered, tested, and reassembled. The resulting set of conceptions, abilities, dispositions, and approaches is what I call each exiting teacher's *professional identity*. Figure 3.1 represents the process graphically.

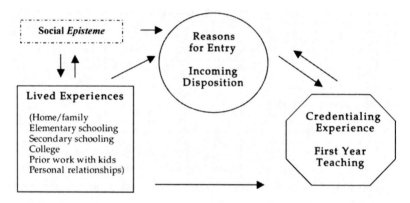

Figure 3.1   Parts and Process of Professional Knowledge Construction

This is the learning process I found. Because the *contents* of each influence strand differed for each teacher, the actual dispositions, conceptions, and resulting experiences and knowledge were also different. This means that, because experience shapes learning and everyone acquires different sets of experience, no individual teacher's knowledge is exactly like another's. But it also means that the *process* by which a teacher constructs professional knowledge is common: The *what* of teacher knowledge varies, but the *how* remains the same. As I have mentioned, I selected the four teachers whose experiences I studied—Azar, William, Kimberly, and Liz—because each attended a different university credentialing program and because they represent the broadest range of fit between candidate and program: William and his program fit well; Kimberly wholly rejected her program; and both Azar and Liz simultaneously accepted and rejected parts of their programs, albeit in different ways.

This chapter conceptualizes beginning teacher development as an individualized product of personal experiences, a sociohistorical enactment of the times, and an effect of one's teacher education experience. Of particular focus is the manner and extent to which each teacher education program interacted with the teacher's incoming disposition.

An Individualized Product of Personal Experiences

In chapter one, I described George Kelly's (1955, 1963) notion of "life themes" as an extension of the philosophies of Kant and Heidegger. Kelly's "constructive alternativism" holds that an individual approaches any experience already in possession of a transparent organizing pattern, or "construct," of the world that is used to perceive, interpret, and make meaning of experience. Each of us creates our particular way of interpreting events—our construct—unconsciously from lived experiences, and so each person possesses what Kelly terms a *life theme*: an intertwined set of biographical events and influences, understandings, and dispositions that acts as an interpretive pattern.[1] The present invokes the past, and both become intertwined; the resulting, fluid knowledge relationships guide the future, which eventually becomes the present, so the process continually repeats.

Applying Kelly's life themes to William, Azar, Kimberly, and Liz allows us to neatly take inventory of ways in which each teacher's past experiences formed interpretive constructs that framed and organized the construction of each of their professional identities. The life themes account not only for the specific way each teacher formed reasons for entering the teaching profession and constructed an incoming set of ideas about teaching, but also for the ways in which each interpreted and processed his or her credentialing program and teaching experiences. Yet no one's experiences exist in a vacuum; instead, they sit inside those particular political, social, cultural, economic, and epistemological features that, in the aggregate, mark any epoch as unique. This leads us into Foucault's *episteme*.

A Sociohistorical Enactment of the Times

Michel Foucault introduced his notion of the *episteme* (from the Greek word for *knowledge*) to suggest that any point in human history is marked by its own distinct collection of political, social, economic, and philo-sophical features, which acts as a kind of epistemology of the times—a boundary of what is knowable, what is allowable, what is considered "true" (Foucault 1970, 1972, 1977). Foucault calls it "the conditions of possibility." For example, until about 240 BC—or as late as AD 1500—the dominant *episteme* within geography (and therefore travel, science, and philosophy) held that the world is flat: To conceive of a spherical planet was outside the bounds of the knowable.

There are identifiable characteristics of the *episteme* that marks our present age—an epoch variously called late modernism, postmodern-ism, globalism, or poststructuralism (Lemert 1997). This period has been described as promoting notions like multiculturalism, heterodoxy, critical theory, the power of emotion, neoliberalism, progress through reason (and, conversely, the rejection of progress through reason), and personal empowerment (Dean 1994; Foucault 1970; Hargreaves 1995; Jameson 1991; Lyotard 1984/1979). There is also a specific climate within the education profession currently that, like an *episteme,* encourages or allows certain ideas about schooling while discouraging, prohibiting, or ignoring others. This notion brings to mind Deborah Britzman's work on how cultural myths and constructions of teaching shape those beginning educators who enter the profession (Britzman 1986, 1991). As well, Thomas Popkewitz's (2001) discussion of "the social administra-tion of the individual" from chapter one, or modern tendencies such as progressivism, constructivism, and the back-to-basics movement, is often invoked to describe recent trends in education (Hirsch 1987; Kozol 1991; Meier 1995; Ravitch 2000; Tyack and Cuban 1995).

Additionally, the current policy landscape of public teaching in the United States (including, but not limited to, the *No Child Left Behind Act*) is marked by increased scrutiny of teachers, high-stakes standard-ized testing, diminishing resources, prescriptive curricula, and a new conception of teacher professionalization (Glickman 2004; McDermott 2007; McGuinn 2006; U.S. Department of Education n.d.). These char-acteristics cannot help but influence educators who exist inside them. In this present study, I found that several currently popularized social notions about education carried indirect influence on the teachers whose experiences I examined: feelings of social obligation, the promise of stu-dent empowerment, a faith in the power of personal experience, a rejec-tion of the psychology of the individual, and a moral-political need for bridging racial and cultural divides. Additionally, I found a presumption on the part of these beginning professionals that success in teaching requires creative and critical thinking—a belief directly at odds with an increasingly prescriptive teaching culture and contemporary emphasis on high-stakes student achievement testing (Meier and Wood 2004). Each of these contemporary assumptions is both a result of and an influence on the current educational epistemology, and they all affected the learning of Azar, Kim, William, and Liz to various extents.

The Formal Teacher Education Experience

William, Kim, Azar, and Liz possessed different kinds of relationships to their credentialing programs. I found each teacher's credentialing relationship to be, itself, multidimensional—existing on three different planes: degree of engagement in program, compatibility with program, and degree of acceptance/rejection of program. For example, William's experience was marked by a high level of engagement with his program, a compatible match, and a high degree of acceptance of his program's knowledge. Kim's experience, on the other hand, was marked by a very low level of engagement (or rather, a high level of disengagement), a fairly compatible match with her program, and a low acceptance (high rejection) of her program's knowledge. Azar's and Liz's experiences had a selective engagement, selective program acceptance, and uneven levels of compatibility with their programs. I use the terms *confirmatory, disconfirmatory,* and *appropriating* to sum up these three dimensions of credentialing relationship.

Confirmatory experiences occurred when a teacher's incoming disposition was mostly aligned with the goals, conceptions, and practices of the credentialing program and the teacher therefore readily accepted the programmatic knowledge. For example, William entered his credentialing program believing that the best learning occurs when students discover or create knowledge themselves. This conception derived from prior experiences: past teachers who modeled and championed such an approach contrasted against those who did not, work experiences as camp counselor and outdoor education instructor, politically radicalizing experiences, and two personal relationships in college. His credentialing program consciously put forth Deweyian, Piagetian, and Vygotskyan versions of constructivism. William, therefore, was predisposed to embrace and begin attaching this programmatic knowledge to his existing ideas and, likewise, adjust his prior conceptions to create a better fit between them and his program. There was no substantive conflict—both were as we might say, "on the same page"—and his program therefore legitimized, gave shape to, and provided a language for his prior ideas. Because the prior disposition matched the experience, two positively correlated changes resulted: The prior conceptions were strengthened by virtue of being confirmed, and the prior conceptions were to some extent altered as the new ideas were accepted and permitted to adjust prior understandings. No dramatic transformation—or "paradigm shift"—occurred, because William was never required to confront or accept a new pattern of thinking.

Disconfirmatory experiences occurred when the beginning teacher encountered a credentialing situation that he or she considered (consciously or not) as opposing previously held personal conceptions and so rejected the program's knowledge. In this case, the learner would confront a set of understandings that, first, did not match the prior beliefs and, second, could not be accepted without fundamentally revising or rejecting the prior beliefs. When this occurred, I found the new set of understandings was rejected, because both ideas could not be simultaneously possessed—to do so would create an unsettling incoherence, a kind of identity dissonance. Interestingly, and unexpectedly, I found no evidence of any teacher rejecting or dramatically transforming prior understandings in the face of new conceptions. The personal always proved stronger than the programmatic. Kimberly, for example, rejected most everything related to her program, for personal reasons that will be discussed later in this chapter.

Appropriating experiences occurred when a beginning teacher interpreted a credentialing situation as neither directly in opposition to nor directly aligned with the teacher's prior conceptions, or as incompatible but not irreconcilable. Because the two knowledge clusters were perceived (by the learner) as different enough, or in some way compatible enough, the learner felt no need to choose between them—there was space for each to exist and for the learner to adjust and fit—or "appropriate"—the credentialing knowledge to his or her prior knowledge. For example, Azar entered her credentialing program with a conception of teaching that strongly emphasized a politicized version of student empowerment. Her program, however, employed a view of student empowerment defined more cognitively. Azar lamented that her program undervalued teaching as a political act, *and* she appreciated the program's emphasis on considering every individual learner's cognitive development. She took her program's emphasis on diagnostic, developmental understandings of learners but selectively altered it to fit her own social justice goals.

Teacher Biographies

Azar

Relatively young, Azar entered teaching at twenty-one. She was born in Iran in 1977. Because her family is Jewish, they immigrated to the United States in 1979 when Khomeini took power. She was raised first in southern California (because there is a strong Iranian community there) and then in a white, upper-middle-class community of northern California where she attended private elementary and high schools and earned a bachelor's degree in psychology from a prestigious public university near her home. Her father is an architect and her mother an accountant; she has two younger sisters. She lived with her family, about whom she spoke lovingly and candidly.

Azar's early experiences (with family, as an immigrant, in school) generated three related teacher purposes: a faith in "community" as educational frame, a sociopolitical emphasis on giving students "voice," and a critical perspective desire for students to "claim their own education." These were important life themes for Azar: the first a *community frame* through which she viewed education, and the second and third a politicized *equity and social justice framework*. Additionally, she strongly valued her personal relationships with teachers and, herself, possessed an informal, highly personable disposition that produced an additional life theme: a *belief in the power of personal, informal relationships* in learning and social settings.

The belief in community began when she was young and appears to be linked to her immigrant experience, her parents, and her schooling. Specifically, it emerged from the difference and social exclusion she experienced being Jewish and Iranian in a white suburb, the closeness she shared with her family, and a conscious move toward friendships with other immigrants:

> It just seems to me, when you're with your culture, your community, they [are the ones who] understand. Like, let's say you like to eat a certain kind

of food, and other cultures see that as sick. But people from your culture understand. I remember when I was growing up—and they didn't have to be my ethnic group, but anyone of color—they could understand why my parents did the things they did. Whereas the whites didn't seem to get that. My friends have always been mostly Latino, Asian, black.

From her parents Azar reported receiving an emphasis on "voice" and "standing up" for what she believes; over time this became an aggressive ideology centered on empowerment. She told me she always "felt listened to" by her parents and was encouraged to "speak her mind" and "debate the issues." She found this a contrast to the larger world:

I was listened to. My parents listened to me, but I always felt that there was a sense of, that when you're a kid your voice is seen as less important. My parents always taught me to voice my opinions ... but I felt like the outside world didn't care because I was a kid.

One of her leitmotifs is the importance of "being heard." In two different interviews a year apart she recounted this same anecdote about her mom at a hardware store:

It started with my parents always telling me to stand up. My mom has always been—like, I remember going to an Orchard Supply store once when I was young, like in middle school I think, and we tried to go in, and it was after closing time, and so she tried to get us in. She's like, "We just need one thing." And the guy's like, "No. There's no way." And so we walked away and then these two women went to the door, and they were blonde. And the guy let them in. And my mom got so pissed off. We're all, "Mom, it's ok, it's ok." But she's all, "No way!" I think she's more aggressive than my dad in a lot of ways. And it's hard because they both have accents. But anyway, she's like, "I don't care. I'm going to fight this." And so we went back up to the store, and she confronted the guy and told him, "I don't think that's fair." He tried to defend himself, but he was kind of stuck because he knew he messed up. Mom said she wanted to talk to the manager, so the manager comes out, and he had to apologize. Told us, "Take as long as you guys need to walk around the store and get anything." So, I think from an early age I was taught to think this way. I had her as a role model. If something is bothering you, you fight. You fight for it. I want my students to see that.

She remembered having to defend her family to her friends and debate them on the merits of her ethnic background—for not being allowed to sleep over at friends' houses when she was young, "because in our culture we don't do that," or for the clothes she wore, or her parents' strictness. Conversely, she told me stories of using debate to convince her parents to ease up on some Iranian customs, like forbidding mixed-gender dances:

> I remember I was in the sixth grade and my parents were all like, "You can't go to this dance, because it's a boy-girl dance." And my dad was really against it. So I fought, and I got to go. My dad let me go, because I used logic to convince him. The fact that I've had to debate a lot in my life has influenced the way I do things.

In high school, Azar found acceptance through academic success. The small, prestigious private school she attended was a close community that valued the kind of serious academics with which she was already comfortable: "Part of [why I felt included there] was because academics was very much a part of the culture. There wasn't a sense of, like, segregation because you like to read, or because you did well." Azar valued the teachers who "related to us as people," "formed a personal connection with a lot of students," or "related to students on more than just a teacher-student relationship." Here, she began to equate effective teaching with forming candid, personal bonds with students and caring about them deeply. She also located her own sociable nature in her family: "It's very personable in my family. Friends come over, and my family's like, 'Stay for dinner! What are you doing these days?' I think that's why it's so easy for me to connect to people."

During her time at the university, Azar underwent a political awakening that radicalized her and ideologized her teaching purposes, and her academic education transformed her personal interest in communities into a conscious philosophy. Specifically, her college experiences as influence on her teacher development fall into six categories: her education minor, her psychology major, her tutoring work, her community outreach participation, her martial arts classes, and the university's political history/climate. Each separately and all of them together strengthened and adjusted her views of community and her desire to effect sociopolitical revolution through teaching. Of particular influence is her community outreach work: Going into local group homes and talking with troubled teenagers forged a link between communities as the useful unit and political empowerment as the primary goal in education and convinced her that marginalized teenagers faced systematic discrimination. Azar was also influenced by the political history on campus. That this university had a celebrated history of political protests and progressivist uprisings infused her own undergraduate experience with revolutionary zeal:

> I don't really know what got me into creating social change. I remember learning about the [history of] protests at [my university] and being like, "Oh, that's so cool!" And then actually getting there in college and being around it and thinking about how there are different ways to instigate social change. Seeing the actual places where the protests occurred. A lot of people were willing to get arrested for their beliefs. I wasn't. I'm a wimp. But I realized I could find other ways to create change.

Directly following college, Azar entered a highly selective teacher credentialing/master's program housed in a local research university. She entered teaching because she wanted to encourage (mostly immigrant) kids to "speak out" and "wanted to let them know someone was listening." She believed this would empower students with both the desire and the tools to effect societal change, thus beginning a kind of revolution. She first thought she would be a psychologist, "because you sit there and listen. You're helping people. And I always felt like kids were never listened to, so that's what I was going to do." But she chose public school teaching, because she believed education was more politically active and less individualistic than psychology; plus, she believed it unfair that as a therapist "you have to charge people [money] to come talk to you."

She chose English because she had always liked to read and write and, during college, suddenly realized that literature did not have to be offputtingly irrelevant:

> The reason I didn't major in English is because I didn't want to take all those boring literature classes with all—like the dead authors from back in the days.... I didn't feel connected to the literature. I loved to read, but [literature was] not representative ethnically or culturally, at all, for the population. To me that turned me off to English. But then I took this [university English] class, and I saw this whole other side of English that I hadn't seen before. I kept thinking, "Wow, if I'd had this in high school, that would have made so much more of an impact."

Azar neither majored nor minored in English (finding literature classes "boring"), although creative writing was one of her two minors. She was not only unhappy with the cultural myopia of the academic canon of literature but also unfamiliar with it and most literary criticism methods as well. Instead, her explanations for teaching were almost always political:

> [Even in high school] I wanted to change things up, but I was too scared then, maybe that's part of it. I want to give students an outlet.... The specific reason I came into education was to help more students, specifically students of color, succeed who aren't working [or being served] in the system. I feel like the system is failing a large proportion of the population, usually the disadvantaged. I feel like it's my community, you know. I struggled a lot because I was an immigrant ... and so my specific target is helping students who normally just kind of slide by, and no one cares.

Kimberly

Kimberly was born in 1960 to a middle-class family in southern California. Neither of her parents went to college; her mother did not finish high school. Her father took over his father's curtain store, and her mom raised the five children. Kim was the middle child among three sisters and a brother. She reported that neither of her parents emphasized school and did not much mind whether or not she graduated from (or even attended) high school. Kim attended a large, comprehensive high school (4,400 students) but almost did not graduate because of low grades and many unexcused absences. After high school she worked for her dad, hanging curtains and working in his shop. For nine years, she held a variety of odd jobs—working in the curtain store, in a hospital, at an insurance company, at a rehabilitation center, and in a day care center for fourteen-year-olds. At twenty-seven she returned to school, because she "was tired of feeling stupid," studying first at local community colleges, then earning a bachelor's degree at a state college and a master's degree in environmental education at the same state university in which, one year later, she would earn her teaching credential.

Her life themes revolve around four notions: a strong emphasis on *fairness and equality,* a view of *her own social existence as a kind of performance,* a belief that *most education is boring,* and her conviction that *teaching is (or should be) easy.* Kimberly told me she believes people receive their values from their parents, and that what she received most was an emphasis on fairness:

This comes not from my credential program but from my mom and dad, maybe having four brothers and sisters. From them I learned how to share. Treating people equally. Not being racist. Not being biased. Not judging people. That's the foundation of me as a teacher. The degree in teaching stuff? The English material you bring in? That's secondary.

Her brother, born with a "deformed arm," was also a catalyst for her beliefs about equality:

His left arm is like half an arm, has a little claw on it, I guess, or whatever. But my mom and dad never treated him differently than any of us. And to this day, my brother can kick your ass in golf. Golfs with one arm. He's really amazing. He has a master's degree. He's a civil engineer. And so the main thing growing up for us was being treated equally.

Kim linked her childhood conceptions of treating people equally to her purposes for teaching: "My whole goal for teaching, I guess, isn't necessarily to teach them, you know, 'Okay, this author wrote this novel, and this was his life,' you know, and blah-blah. Mine really is to make them more open-minded and more accepting of differences, like what my parents taught me."

She had always wanted to be a stand-up comic and explained that her position as middle child produced in her a need for attention:

[Part of what I enjoy about teaching is] the performance aspect. Very much. That it's all about me, because I want to be a stand-up comic. I mean, come on! It's a total, secret goal of mine, and this is the closest I will ever get to that. The more they laugh at my jokes, the more I like them.... Sometimes I jump on the desk, and I'll yell [the announcements] out at the top of my lungs. I want them to be on the edge of their seat.

BRAD: Where does this longing to be a stand-up comedian come from?

KIM: Oh my God. From, like, the time I was like twelve, I think. You haven't noticed that I'm total center-of-attention? Total center-of-attention. If you laugh at me, you will be my best friend. I think it comes seriously from my family. I'm in the middle out of five kids. Totally need attention. I'll do anything for a laugh ... my older sister used to totally egg me on, like on a daily basis. And she would egg me on, and then I would get attention from her, and I would get attention from my brother, and I need it.

About elementary school, she could only remember talking a lot, making jokes, and earning attention from students and teachers alike:

> I remember always getting in trouble for talking. They wanted to do psychological testing on me [for excessive talking], but my mom refused and said, "There's absolutely nothing wrong with her. She just likes to talk. Get over it." I mean, I would talk to anybody. Anybody that would listen. And get everybody else talking. I just have this persona; like, in a meeting, I could get you to talk and laugh when I'm not supposed to. On my kindergarten report card, it says, you know, "Kimberly, basically, won't shut up." I was voted class clown in eighth grade.

Kimberly believed that a confluence of three factors explains her mostly unpleasant high school experience: boring teachers, a demeanor more suited for play and social attention than academic study, and parents who were not concerned with school. Connecting her own students to her experiences in school, Kim explained,

> Oh my God, absolutely; my experience in high school affects how I see these kids. I definitely relate to these [lowest tracked twelfth grade] students, because in high school I was them. I had a 1.6 grade point average in high school. I was a ditcher. I didn't want to be in high school; I hated it. My parents were not big into high school; they didn't really push it. It was okay if I didn't go. I was like [my students]. And when you're seventeen, eighteen, you know, you don't give a shit about high school; you just don't care.

Kim presumed teaching was relatively easy. She told me teaching is "eighty percent common sense," and was best learned by "just jumping in and doing it." She said that a teacher can teach skills he or she does not possess: "As long as you've got passion for it, you should be allowed to teach [any subject]. You can teach somebody the skills without you yourself being able to do them well."

At twenty-seven, Kim returned to school, first studying at several local community colleges, then earning a bachelor's degree in English: "When I was in community college a teacher said, 'You're a good writer; you should keep writing.' So I got an English degree, not really knowing why." She reported returning to school because she no longer wanted to feel stupid at social gatherings:

You go to these parties where—you know, work parties and such. I felt so stupid. I could not compete. I couldn't have an intelligent conversation with someone, and I thought—I was convinced it was because I never went to college. You know, I was just a screw-off in high school: "I need to really think about things here, what am I gonna, you know, how am I gonna have an intelligent conversation with someone?" And it was like, "Oh, I get it. I have to go back to school." So, by the time that rolled around I was twenty-seven.

After moving up to northern California and then being laid off from an insurance job, Kim began looking for work and found employment as a substitute teacher. Eventually, she got a long-term assignment at a nearby high school and simultaneously—because she thought she wanted to start her own summer camp—studied in an environmental education master's program. A year later she enrolled in the credentialing program at the same commuter university where she had just earned her MEd.

William

William was born in upstate New York in 1974 to middle-class parents. His father—the first in his own family to attend college—was a trial lawyer who traveled the state defending doctors, often bartering for his services: William remembered him once coming back with a horse as payment. His mom stayed at home to raise William and his younger sister. William was raised with a Catholic sense of social obligation and his father's stern work ethic. He attended the local elementary school, working and attending camp each summer, and for high school went away to a private boarding school, which he grew to loathe. He attended a small liberal arts college in Maine, majoring in English and enjoying the intellectual rigor, political activism, and the many outdoor opportunities it afforded. After college, he moved to northern California with his girlfriend.

William's life themes concern a strong sense of *social obligation*; a conviction that *learning is discovery and creating knowledge*; an *intellectual, critical stance toward the consumerism, discrimination, and deforestation inherent in today's society*; and a *love for the energy and curiosity of youth*. He attributed his social obligation to two strands of his experience. One is his parents becoming "radicalized Catholics" when he was young:

I'm still a recovering Catholic. I was brought up with all these ideas of social obligation. Serving dinners in shelters during Thanksgiving, having ministry workers staying at the house ... and in the end I know that the democratic ideal of teaching is for me. I wouldn't be happy doing something else.

The other is his several years at a progressivist summer camp that championed living the examined life, caring for the environment, and helping others: "The idea of an examined life became really important to me. Reflection—you know, reflecting on your life. For me this led to a [politically] liberal point of view. Community responsibility. Helping others. Learning by doing."

In school, William reported being influenced by two teachers who "both taught very nontraditionally in terms of [students] creating [their own] knowledge ... and I would love to somehow make my classes hit home that way." During college, William came to believe that minority populations were discriminated against; this set in motion a reflective process that led to a reconsideration of his past and an emergent critical consciousness:

> I went to [a high school that was] a bastion of conservative elitism. And I kind of knew the place was messed up, and going to college I got some theory behind what I was feeling. Studying to be a critical thinker, I began to question a lot. My time at [college] really gave me the tools to examine why [my private high school] was messed up. [My camp experiences] gave me the beginning tools, and then, college really, you know—that's where you begin to break it down. Like, why things are so fucked up and how women get treated or homophobia at the school. And the fact that very few of the kids of color could ever graduate [from my high school]. All those issues started to make sense when I was in college. My girlfriend is a woman of color, and we went to college together, and we talk about how, like for her, college was a radicalizing experience. There's something of a white, straight privilege going on. College was great for me, you know—I could get by. Straight white guy, some intelligence, some athleticism. But my big learning process was realizing that it wasn't great for a lot of people. It was a pretty shitty place for a lot of people.

He majored in English and brought an intellectually rigorous approach to the study of literary theory and poetry, even spending a term abroad studying a small group of poets in Ireland.

William's enthusiasm for and enjoyment with youth ("I love the fun of kids. I get a kick out of them.") originated in his many summer camp experiences and took shape during two years' work with young people after college (as a county naturalist leading school tours, as a youth program coordinator and tutor): "I like spending time with kids, or joking with kids. Because, for me, if I don't have that [fun, joking] part of the experience it would be dry."

He chose teaching, because he loved English and literature, wanted to assist young people in reaching their goals, and because "I just get a lot of energy from kids. They keep me moving ... just the enthusiasm and the fun I have with them. Eventually, there was also the desire and feeling that I had things I wanted to share, but that was always in the context of having a good time." He entered his credentialing program with the beliefs that teaching is difficult but can be mastered over time ("It's hard but isn't magic—I'll get good at it eventually."), that students learn best by discovering their own knowledge, that classroom safety and comfort precede learning, and that issues of race and culture should be made explicit in the curriculum.

Liz

Because the previous chapter presented an extended discussion of Liz, here I will only briefly review her biography. Liz was born in 1970, and grew up in Staten Island, New York. Her English teacher father proved to be a powerful influence on Liz's interest in and ideas about teaching. Her mother was also a teacher for a short time, and one of her two older brothers was studying to be a college English professor. Education, she reported, was the "family business." Liz attended public schools, including a performing arts high school (as a trumpet player), and studied briefly at Barnard College and a New York City community college before moving to San Francisco. In the Bay Area, she worked full-time in a bookstore for three years, played in a rock band, and earned her bachelor's degree in English at the same state university in which she ultimately received her teaching credential. She had no prior experiences working with children.

Her life themes include a love of and commitment to literature and English grammar, a social justice desire to provide marginalized populations (defined socioeconomically) access to success through quality teaching, and a dual insider/outsider social perspective consciously manifested as an emphasis on "coolness."

The Credentialing Programs

Although I did collect available recruiting and program information for the four credentialing programs, I do not make much use of them here. I found their content to be largely symbolic—designed to suggest everything one could hope for in teacher education: cutting-edge teaching methodologies, humanist principles, rigorous intellectual experiences, exceptional staff. All programs trumpeted supportive yet challenging experiences for beginners en route to becoming educational leaders destined for success with diverse learners. Instead, I made use of this information for organizational details but relied on my observation and interview data to identify the approaches and characteristics of each preparation program.

University of Weber Teacher Education Program—Azar

The Weber program was medium sized, highly selective, and expensive. The eleven-month program began in the summer, when teacher candidates co-taught (with veteran teachers) a middle school summer session and took university classes, and continued through fall and spring semesters as candidates student-taught two classes in one of the local high schools while taking university courses. Each candidate's student teaching was overseen by the two cooperating teachers whose classrooms the candidate took over and a university supervisor—typically a veteran teacher or doctoral student working part-time at Weber. The courses were taught by university professors and program lecturers and fell into two categories: required courses (including curriculum and instruction; teaching, learning, and motivation; and technology in the classroom) and a series of electives (including bilingualism, perspectives on teaching, and cooperative learning). Students who successfully completed all requirements earned both their secondary teaching credential and their MAT.

Weber put forward a finely researched, progressivist vision of teaching and learning that focused on practitioner reflection, student meaning-making, diagnostic understandings of adolescents and learning, cooperative instruction, authentic assessment, and differentiated instruction. As the program director told me, Weber believes that

> a beginning teacher needs to know about students—about kids, about their development and the way that gets played out in their lives.... And they need to know their content—what they're teaching about.... [And]

Table 3.1   Program Matrix for Weber University

Type	• Credentialing and master's • All subject areas
Length	• 11 months (July to May)
Size	• 72 students, approx. 18 staff
Admissions	• Highly selective • $12,000 tuition
Structure	• Student teaching summer, fall, and spring terms. • Required and elective university courses (see "Courses" below). • University supervisor, school site cooperating teachers, weekly supervisory meetings. • Weekly seminar meetings.
Courses	Curriculum and instruction in English, education, and the U.S. Constitution; adolescent development and learning; group work for heterogeneous classrooms.
Staff	• Education professors and lecturers; graduate students and veteran teachers as supervisors. • Conscious attempt to use cooperating teachers whose teaching philosophies match Weber's
Characteristics	• Heavy emphasis on theory and research, especially developmental understandings of students and application of cooperative learning strategies. • Focus on pre-service teachers as successful learners in need of diagnostic understandings of student development and corresponding teaching strategies. • Emphasis on individual differences among children; little attention to cultural or ethnic difference among students or teachers. • Because program housed in a larger school of education, candidates exposed to other graduate education perspectives and resources.

they need a beginning group of strategies for teaching ... enough of an array so that they can begin to match the strategy for the situation.... And a beginning respect for their profession, and an ethical base for the moral part of teaching. Those are the major things.

Gould University Teacher Education Program—Kimberly

The Gould program was a relatively inexpensive, unselective, ten-month single-subject internship program in which candidates taught as paid interns teaching two to five classes per day in one of the nearby high schools for an academic year while attending university courses in the evenings. Each candidate ostensibly had a university supervisor scheduled to observe the teacher twice monthly and an intern support provider in place of a cooperating teacher, yet Kim reported having no intern support provider, and she found her supervisor ineffectual ("All he does is tell me how great I am. That doesn't help me."). The program was medium-sized (about thirty-five students in each cohort, several cohorts studying concurrently) and accepted candidates from across the disciplines.

Talking with me, the cohort director emphasized nuts-and-bolts teaching skills and strategies, especially classroom management ("Because if the room is berserk, they can't ever try any of the wonderful ideas they have."), and planning lessons around learning standards ("which are coming down from everywhere and from every politician"). This director reported that Gould privileged concrete teaching skills and strategies over theoretical understandings and research perspectives:

> We aren't heavy on a lot of theory attached to gurus' names. I mean, I don't think the folks on my team could cite people by name and their theories. That's not where we are ... we leave that to the master's program.

It appeared to me that the Gould program did not present one unified, coherent theory of teaching but rather reflected the "structural fragmentation" Kenneth Zeichner and Daniel Liston (1990) have previously discussed, and was assembled out of the idiosyncratic, or "balkanized" (Hargreaves 1995), educational approaches of staff members and "added-on" components. Many program lecturers were veteran teachers or district administrators who relied on their own professional experiences for their curriculum and instruction and, because most were part-time instructors, came to campus only for their evening classes; this meant

Table 3.2 Program Matrix for Gould University

Type	• Credentialing • All subject areas
Length	• 11 months (July to May)
Size	• Approx. 135 students divided into cohorts, 20–25 staff
Admissions	• Not selective • $2,600 tuition
Structure	• Intern teaching fall and spring terms. • Required university courses that met weekly (some for full semester, others smaller "module" courses). • University supervisor, intern support provider (latter not present). • No weekly seminar meetings.
Courses	Multicultural education, psychological foundations, classroom management, planning instruction, disciplinary methods, social/cultural influences.
Staff	• Education professors and instructors; veteran teachers hired as part-time lecturers. No information on-site supervisors.
Characteristics	• Structural fragmentation—little coherence among program components, no unified program culture. • Little reliance on theory or education research; instead, an emphasis on transferring instructors' wisdom of practice and concrete teaching ideas to teacher candidates. • Presumed intern teaching to be educational crux, and program component merely a way to facilitate the internship practicum: Teachers will learn best by teaching.

there were few program meetings or opportunities for staff to talk and plan collaboratively.

Frederic University Master's
in Teaching English Program—William

The Frederic program was small, selective, moderately expensive, and housed inside a large research university. Frederic University's program was designed solely for teachers of English and was composed of equal parts theory and practitioner wisdom (and attempts to integrate them). Students took three terms (summer, fall, and spring) of required university classes, including urban education, language study for educators, and educational psychology, and met weekly for an intensive English methods seminar co-taught by the program directors. Students fulfilled their practicum duties by teaching one class in a middle school fall semester and two classes in a high school spring semester, overseen in both cases by cooperating teachers and university supervisors. Successful completion of the first year earned graduates a single-subject English teaching credential with a cross-cultural, language, and academic development (CLAD) emphasis. During the second year, the credentialed teachers met biweekly, and each completed a master's thesis to earn an MAT.

The program drew heavily from education research and put forward an approach to teaching and learning that relied on three related traditions of inquiry: constructivism, multiculturalism, and sociocultural theories of English development. The program stressed the belief that effective teaching is developmental, reflective, and best conducted in accordance with theoretical understandings adjusted to fit contextual particulars. One of the codirectors explained:

You don't [ever] stop learning to teach, because every kid is different, every context is different. [Beginning teachers] need to feel confidence in knowing a body of work, in terms of what their discipline is. And then they have to realize that there is another body of scholarship that they're novices in, which is the scholarship of teaching and learning. So they may have extremely high levels of expertise in their content, extremely high standards for themselves and their students, and high commitments towards issues around equity, and yet they are infants in the world of how to create the environment in which there's both the subject area and the sort of values and community [that] can be combined in a powerful way.

Table 3.3   Program Matrix for Frederic University

Type	• Credentialing and MAT • English/ESL subject only, CLAD emphasis
Length	• 2 years (1 year intensive, 1 year to write master's thesis)
Size	• 17 students, 8 staff
Admissions	• Highly selective • $6,000 tuition
Structure	• Student teaching fall and spring terms. • Required university courses summer, fall, spring terms. • University supervisor, school site cooperating teachers; courses met weekly. • Weekly seminar meetings. • Second-year master's requirement: biweekly meetings and thesis submission.
Courses	Urban education, reading development, English and ESL teaching methods, educational psychology, language study for educators.
Staff	• Education professors and instructors, graduate student supervisors and lecturers; veteran teachers as supervisors and seminar guests.
Characteristics	• Heavy reliance on theory and research, especially constructivism and Deweyan conceptions of experience and education. • Mix of "lessons from the classroom" and theoretical perspectives on teaching and learning. • Small program meant for informal relations among staff and students, collaborative feel; collegiality stressed. • Considered teaching a political as well as academic and social act. • Because program housed in larger school of education, candidates exposed to other graduate education perspectives and resources.

Casals University Teacher Education Program—Liz

The program at Casals was unselective, inexpensive, and large (one of the largest credentialing programs in the state). The ten-month program consisted of two semesters: The first entailed a series of university courses and school site observations, and the second one entailed the second half of the methods seminar and a student teaching practicum. The crux of the coursework was a fall semester curriculum and instruction in the content area class, and a yearlong teaching methods seminar (across the disciplines). For the student teaching component, candidates assumed

Table 3.4   Program Matrix for Casals University

Type	• Single-subject credential, CLAD optional; for candidates of most subject areas
Length	• 1 academic year
Size	• 6 cohorts of approximately 20 students each
Admissions	• Relatively unselective • $3,000 tuition
Structure	• Observations fall term, student teaching spring term. • Required university courses fall term. Weekly seminar meetings both semesters. • University supervisor, school site cooperating teachers; courses met weekly.
Courses	Teaching methods, curriculum, and instruction; the Constitution; reading development.
Staff	• Education professors and lecturers; full-time teachers as cooperating teachers.
Characteristics	• Some structural fragmentation. • Mostly "lessons from the classroom" and concrete teaching strategies. • Considered teaching a political as well as academic and social act. Emphasis on acknowledging cultural difference. Antiracist teaching. • Because program built around the methods seminar, the seminar instructor (who is also practicum coordinator and supervisor) is quite influential.

the principal teaching duties in two classes at one middle or high school, overseen by a university supervisor and cooperating teachers.

As discussed previously, the program put forth a set of conceptions loosely linked by their adherence to student-centered instructional tenets, a social view of learning, and emphasis on concrete methods rather than theoretical framings of teaching and learning.

Life Themes and Teacher Knowledge Construction

To examine the ways each teacher's personal history interacted with his or her teacher education program, I have divided teacher knowledge into three categories: conceptions of/dispositions toward subject, conceptions of/dispositions toward students, and conceptions of/dispositions toward teaching and learning. Though other researchers segment teacher knowledge differently (Elbaz [1981] into five categories, Grossman [1990] into four categories, Leinhardt and Greeno [1985] into two, and Shulman [1986a, 1987] into seven), I found a tripartite grouping separate enough for analysis yet whole enough for ecological viewing. In the three subsections that follow, I examine each teacher's knowledge with an eye toward the holistic, recursive, personal-programmatic principles that shaped its development.

Conceptions of Subject

Azar and Kimberly were more interested in teaching life lessons than academic or disciplinary content. William was equally interested in both. Liz was mostly interested in teaching disciplinary content. These framings of the teaching of English derived in each case from conceptions that resulted from interrelations among life themes and program experiences.

The many contours of relationship between teachers' subject conceptions and their teaching have been well examined (Darling-Hammond, Wise, and Klein 1995; Grossman 1990; Grossman, Wilson, and Shulman 1989; Gudmundsdottir and Shulman 1987; Lampert and Ball 1998; Shulman 1987). Subject knowledge particulars shape a teacher's ways of interpreting student questions and student work; and they shape a teacher's curricular goals, lesson plans, and even the subtle manner in which any teacher represents his or her personal relationship with, and therefore implied importance of, curricular material. My study revealed that, first, the teachers drew heavily on their life themes in conceiving of their subject and, second, their specific subject conceptions and prior subject learning experiences significantly influenced their teaching.

Generally, Azar and Kim viewed English as a subject solely as a means, not an end. They both viewed English as a way to introduce various "life lessons" and encourage political or personal (Azar and Kim, respectively) development in students. William saw English as both an end and a means; as a valuable discipline loaded with inherently valuable texts and skills to learn; and as a developmental forum in which—through discussion and reflection—students could become comfortable with school learning, grow further into thoughtful individuals, and earn social capital through literacy. Liz saw it as mostly an aesthetic and cultural tradition, as an honorable academic discipline of literature and language whose mastery was required if one were to be successful in life and aesthetically complete.

Regarding these conceptions of English, each candidate had a different credentialing relationship. William's was confirmatory. He matriculated with an incoming set of conceptions that included a strong social justice view of education and a faith in—and personal experience with—empowerment through education. William also possessed a strong academic background in English and social theory, a passion for literature, and a background in which knowing literature and standard English had opened up social, personal, and economic opportunities for him. That his credentialing program was solely for English (and ESL) teacher candidates meant that all the teaching theories, models, and conversations were specifically about the teaching of English, and most peer talk concerned English teaching. This created a powerful scaffold inside of which William could interpret and experiment with his program's knowledge. Additionally, while stressing English as a discipline, his program simultaneously recognized nonacademic dimensions of student learning. This acknowledgment allowed William to employ his social justice frame without conflict. This means that because he and his program considered high school English both an academic discipline and a discursive space for the further sociopolitical development of children, they fit, and each mostly confirmed the other. Because his program was solely for English teacher candidates, he was immersed in pedagogical content knowledge. And because—from high school and college—he was already comfortable thinking theoretically, he was quick to embrace his program's heavy reliance on theory and research.

Azar, Kim, and Liz attended credentialing programs for candidates across subject disciplines and therefore had less direct exposure to English subject knowledge, pedagogical content knowledge, or English methods (Azar and Liz had some; Kim had almost none). This means it was left for each of them privately to apply to English many of the theories and strategies they were offered. It also means that their subject backgrounds (weak, in the cases of Azar and Kim) went mostly unexposed either to themselves or their programs. Though they both, like many beginning teachers, felt insecure about their subject knowledge in the classroom, neither felt it was severe, and both expected to learn their subject as they taught it. Further, as I will soon explain, Kim was disposed to reject most anything her program presented; this means that even if her program had addressed her particular conceptions of subject, she would not have heard it.

Weber did offer partial confirmation of Azar's nonacademic goals for the teaching of English. Her program approved of teachers considering English not only as a discipline but also as developmental tool and social currency whose mastery invites power and resources. However, Azar's strong adherence to a political view of education caused her to believe her program stopped short. She often complained that Weber overemphasized academics and college preparedness and underemphasized issues of race, class, and social justice in education. Additionally, the data suggest that Azar might have been stressing social justice in part to compensate for her subject matter weakness; if it is true that we tend to emphasize what we know, then it is likely that Azar felt more confident relying on her strongest life theme, even leveraging it as a complaint against the more traditional notions of subject matter she perceived her program to embrace.

For Kim, the credentialing relationship was disconfirmatory, even though her program was, in fact, more or less compatible with her incoming disposition on this (both shared emphases on functional fluency, moral fairness, and encouraging students to enjoy literature). From the beginning Kim had decided her program was useless. There are several reasons for this, and together they account for her decision to (1) dislike the program and (2) actively reject learning from it. One reason is that she felt bitter that, having just earned an MEd, she had to return to school to become credentialed ("I did it backwards and I know that. My mind-set was, 'I'm done with school,' so I went in there with a really poor attitude, and it has stuck."). A second is that she had never felt comfortable or successful in school—though I do not have sufficient data to be certain, this credentialing experience probably dredged up some past unpleasantness. And the third reason is that Kim instantly disliked her cohort director:

> I hate her so much. She is the most condescending person I've ever met in my whole life.... I think she's the world's biggest bitch. I've never felt that about anybody else, really. I thought that from the very first day. I had an interview with her. She made me feel so stupid and so uneducated.

Notice that the final two reasons for disliking the program appear to derive at least in part from her feelings of insecurity—strong evidence supporting claims that self-concept, motivation, and learning are intertwined (Csikszentmihalyi 1991; Krashen 1987; Schiefele 1991). Kim's initial disengagement from the program was itself confirmed—and therefore reinforced—during the yearlong experience, because her one friend in the program also rejected it and because colleagues at her school had recounted their own disappointing credentialing experiences.

Interestingly, Liz had more knowledge of, and a stronger interest in, the subject of English than did her program. This came from her father as primary teacher model and her many positive experiences with the study of English as a discipline. In her program, Liz found no confirmation of her interest in teaching grammar, the English canon, and literary analysis. Liz interpreted her program—which stressed cooperative learning and social development perspectives—as ignoring content mastery in favor of student comfort, and she resisted programmatic attempts to adjust her thinking. She strongly believed the teacher, as disciplinary expert, has an obligation to deliver content to students who learn from the teacher's knowledge. She viewed acceptance of the student-centered model a rejection of the teacher-as-expert and, therefore, a rejection of her father-as-model. Liz spent much of the fall semester distancing herself from her father's model of teaching and simultaneously accepting her father's influence, not sure what conclusions to draw. This ambivalence created an uncomfortable struggle for Liz: There were ways in which she wanted to accept her program's approach, but she believed that to do so meant fully rejecting her prior conceptions (and her father's influence).

Conceptions of Students

Azar and Kimberly viewed their students through the lens of their own biographies. William conceived of his students as being dramatically unlike himself. Liz began by presuming her students were like herself but reframed her conceptions to emphasize differences between her and her students. These framings of students derived in the cases of Azar, Kimberly, and Liz from an interrelation among previous experiences, and in William from hyperconscious attention to difference.

Teachers make tacit decisions about students when setting goals; designing curriculum; planning, implementing, and evaluating lessons; looking at student work; and interacting with students in or outside the classroom. This means that the ways teachers understand their students affect their teaching on multiple levels. Teachers often presume their students resemble themselves (Jackson 1986). They rely on various sociocultural generalizations regarding race, language, culture, gender, and class as they interpret and interact with students (Avery and Walker 1993; Barry and Lechner 1995; McIntosh 1988; Tatum 1999). I found that Azar, Kimberly, William, and Liz all tended to consider students in relation to themselves and their own backgrounds; for Azar, Kimberly, and Liz, the relationship was positively correlated, and for William the relation was an inverse one.

Employing what Philip Jackson (1986) termed *presumption of shared identity*, Azar viewed her students through her own biographical lens. This means that when her students were immigrants (and most of them were), she presumed their immigrant experience was like hers. Interestingly, however, Azar never acknowledged two significant differences: her parents' educational histories and her family's socioeconomic position. Azar presumed her students' parents' resources in education resembled her own. Yet, her own parents—with more education, professional careers, and economically comfortable lives in the United States (even sending their children to private schools)—might, in fact, have viewed educational success as more valuable or attainable than the typically working- or lower-middle-class parents, often without much formal education, to which Azar compared them.[2] Also, Azar's social location as an upper-middle-class young person, raised in a mostly comfortable suburb, most likely disposed her views of the world in ways different from many of her students. And, finally, because Azar never acknowledged differences between her own private high school and the large, underfunded public school in which she taught, we can presume she ignored substantive variations that can differentiate thriving from troubled high schools (Bryk, Lee, and Holland 1993; Kozol 1991) and ways in which this distinguished her immigrant experience from that of her students (Quiocho and Rios 2000; Au and Blake 2003).

The Weber program appeared to ignore the unique experiences of cultural minority members who enter teaching. Alice Quiocho and Francisco Rios (2000) reviewed 476 studies conducted over the last decade to find that cultural minority upbringings often carry powerful influence on minority teachers. One example is Rene Galindo (1996), who found immigrant teachers more likely to become change agents in their schools. For Azar this was certainly true, yet because her program did not address this and other influences from her cultural positioning, she was left to retain the construct unchallenged. She did not, to my knowledge, problematize her schooling differences against theirs, investigate differences among immigrant groups, or examine the insider-outsider distinction from her own "insider" perspective. This was one of those unchallenged influences, scuttled in under the rug, that became part of Azar's teacher knowledge.

Like Azar, Kim viewed her students through her own biographical lens. This meant three things: (1) She saw her twelfth grade students (the lowest-tracked course, called "community college English," because that was where they were presumably headed) as versions of herself, (2) she saw her tenth grade students ("honors" track) as entirely unlike her, and (3) she relied on her personality and experiences as her primary teaching guide. Kim had found her own high school boring. And she was frequently truant and did poorly in her classes. She told me she wanted "to be the teacher I wish I had in high school for the kind of student I was." With her twelfth grade students, therefore, she was entertaining and academically undemanding. Conversely, Kimberly distanced herself from her tenth grade honors classes, adopting a more formalized teacher stance and frequently lecturing off published notes, assigning expository essays, and administering question-and-answer tests. She also told me that around her tenth graders she felt her lack of subject knowledge more acutely—and, of course, this cannot be overlooked: Her discomfort with these students must derive as much from feelings of professional inadequacy as from perceived personal or age differences.

The Gould University program was partially confirmatory for Kim to the extent that she paid attention to it. Gould's approach to pedagogy loosely corresponded to Kim's way of treating her twelfth grade students: Understand from where your students are coming, be yourself as a teacher—anything else is unnatural and will not work. I think her program professors would be pleased that she made jokes in class, acted natural (its oxymoron notwithstanding), and formed personal relationships with students. The program appeared never to have exposed candidates to negative consequences of this overreliance on self (Britzman 1986, 1991; Jackson 1986). Regarding her tenth grade students, had her subject knowledge been stronger, she might have felt more confident—and therefore more comfortable—with these academically minded students. If she had been forced to reflect closely on possible sources and alternative reasons for her students' varied levels of inclination toward school, she might have determined that biography is not always the best guide.

William approached the conceiving of his students methodically and scientifically. His predisposition was to be analytical and reflective, and his program taught him theories of learning, literacy development, and the effects of cultural difference. He therefore self-consciously attempted to align his understanding of students with the research he was learning: He lowered expectations and distanced students from himself. Interestingly, though, William had analyzed himself into a corner. The more he "studied" minority youth—framing them as an "other"—the more he distanced them from himself and his biography. This appears to be a kind of pathologizing of difference. Yet, because William simultaneously believed in the educational benefits of personal connections with students and a comfortable classroom, there was conflict between his goal of intimacy and a perceived hyper-difference.[3]

William's experience with the Frederic program was confirmatory in this respect, with one caveat. The confirmatory part is that he unproblematically embraced his program's theoretical, researched understandings of literacy theory, adolescent development, and the study of race, class, and culture as he got to know his students. He accounted for race, class, culture, reading level, maturation, and personality variations. He always stressed the positive, even as he lowered expectations and shifted individual agency back and forth, on and off, students. These were precisely the ideas his program championed and presented to students. Yet, there is an interesting extent to which this thinking might carry a person. Like Lisa Delpit (1995) who fears that white, middle-class teachers can unintentionally frame African-American students inside a deficit model, so, too, is there a *next level* of unintentional framing. By this I mean that William was so hypersensitively aware of ways in which African-American urban kids are *demonized* (his word) that he, it seems, moved to the opposite side of the spectrum: He was so willing to champion the virtues of African-American urban youth that he all but placed them out of his reach. At this point in his professional development, he had convinced himself he could never enter their worlds, gain their respect, teach them—at one point telling me he viewed himself as a "speed bump" hindering their development. This distance affected his teaching, creating in the classroom what I interpreted as a palpable, awkward sense of difference between William and his students.

To understand her students, Liz appeared to rely on the most relevant set of conceptions she believed she possessed: memories of her own schooling. Like Azar and Kim, she presumed her students were like herself. This meant that she believed they would enjoy learning once they saw the value of it; would respond to a "cool" teacher who liked rock-and-roll, cracked jokes, respected adolescents, and wore denim pants; came from families engaged in and supportive of academic learning; and learned best through didactic demonstration. Instead, she found students unwilling to respect her authority; politely refusing to do homework; reporting that they did not receive much academic encouragement from home; and uninterested in maintaining a personal, rock-and-roll rapport with her. Further, she was shocked by what she considered their active resistance to standardized English usage. Liz's experience teaching was in large part an exercise in lowering her expectations of students while still preserving her optimism in students and subtly shifting responsibility off herself and them and onto failing schools and a discriminatory society.

Liz had an appropriating relationship with her program in respect to conceptions of students. Her program professors encouraged Liz to acknowledge effects of structural discrimination on student behavior and learning in the classroom. Her seminar leader promoted antiracist teaching (McIntosh 1988; Tatum 1999). This emphasis on culture, class, race, and privilege, however, provided a difficult tension for someone like Liz, whose prior conceptions were steeped inside traditional, academic-based ideas of teaching: Liz tried to reconcile her incoming desire to hold students to rigorous academic and behavioral standards with her newfound understanding that years of multifaceted discrimination require a special kind of sensitivity toward students. She accepted that her urban students were unlike the suburban ones her father had taught, and she wanted to embrace her program's philosophy. But her distaste for the decreased learning, lowered expectations, and wasted time she believed attended cooperative learning approaches made her conclude her program framed students inside a deficit model. This binary opposition structured her interesting interpretation of Lisa Delpit (1995) as offering her a way to preserve her dad's knowledge transfer view of students yet remain sensitive to "other people's children." As I recounted in chapter one, Liz told me, "[Delpit] did this great thing at the beginning of ['The Silenced Dialogue'], which was something like, I found out that a child can learn from being constantly corrected and not end fucked-up, or something like that."

Conceptions of Teaching and Learning

Teaching Goals. All four teachers conceived of teaching and learning with an emphasis on student empowerment, but each teacher possessed different variations. Azar believed students should be provided with rich opportunities to reflect, discuss, and articulate, and that whatever results should be considered valuable learning. Kim believed that students should have fun, think hard, and learn what the teacher tells them. William was a strong believer in students making their own meaning. Liz believed she could best empower students by ensuring they learn English language and literature well.

Teaching Style. Azar's informal disposition and her emphasis on personal relationships and political activism shaped her style. Kim's relationships with colleagues and her belief that effective teachers are performers who keep student boredom at bay informed her pedagogy. William's heightened attention to race, economics, and power shaped his teaching, and informed both his idea of constructivism and his emphasis on student safety. Liz's pedagogy was structured as an uneasy hybrid of didactic instruction and student-centered group work.

Azar

Azar's life themes led her to an incoming view of teaching and learning that was both political and constructivist. Her emphasis on "voice" and her insistence that students "claim their own education" engendered a politicized version of constructivism different from but compatible with the cooperative learning, teach-for-understanding curriculum her credentialing program advocated:

> Students obtain knowledge by interacting with it. For example, I asked my students to define what a teacher was and what a student was. And it was interesting how some of them would say, "A student is like a sponge—soaks up the knowledge the teacher gives it." And others would be like this little rebel and say, "The student isn't there to say what the teacher wants; the student does whatever they want." And I guess that [the latter one] is a definition I agree with.

This empowerment-minded conception of student as meaning-maker, of successful students as courageous constructivists, fits well with the student-centered, cooperative learning Weber endorsed, and Azar was quick to attach her political and community education goals to her program's developmental teaching strategies. But Azar's own personal history was never far from her professional understandings; notice, for example, her reliance on martial arts as she fashioned this constructivist teaching analogy:

> It's like in my martial arts classes, they tell us, "This is the way the technique is." And they'll say, "Different people will do it different ways. And depending on your height, your weight, or your ability, you're going to change it yourself." So when you gain the knowledge of that technique, you cannot do it the same way you're taught it, because you're different from the person who taught you it. So you have to adapt it. And a teacher, I feel, is someone who allows that process of gaining knowledge to occur that way.

Azar recognized that lecturing is sometimes necessary, though she reported hating it (and I never observed her lecture). She was constantly exclaiming in class, "It's your education! Claim it!" She employed a rubric system of grading so as to eliminate A–F grades and demystify assessment, and turned over some of the evaluative power to students. And she almost never offered her opinions in class, preferring to ask questions and, as cheerleader, encourage students to create their own ideas.

Azar believed her students wanted a personal, caring, informal teacher, because this was what she had appreciated in high school. And her life themes led her to an incoming highly politicized view of teaching and learning. From her undergraduate peer tutoring work, she was accustomed to relating to students the way she related to peers. Her psychology coursework in college confirmed her belief that making personal connections with students was good teaching, and so Azar saw no reason not to be her own informal, hip-hop-oriented self in the classroom. The Weber program, encouraging teachers to use their personalities to connect with students and make the classroom a natural, comfortable place, confirmed Azar's incoming disposition. Azar used slang and the hip-hop discourse of contemporary adolescent culture, and she accepted it from her students. She preferred that students call her "Azar" rather than use her surname for several intertwined reasons—all of them consistent with her life themes: (1) University tutoring had made her familiar with a first-name basis, (2) "it feels fake to be impersonal," (3) it encouraged personal relationships, and (4) she believed it empowered students by further flattening the classroom hierarchy.

Kim

The primary influences on Kim's views of teaching and learning were her own schooling experiences, her conceptions of students, her professional satisfaction (and ease), her teacher friends at the school, and the forge of classroom trial-and-error. The role of these influences remained unchanged by her programmatic experience. Kim's program had almost no influence on her pedagogical knowledge. She rejected learning from program peers ("They're all inexperienced people. They're just as lost as I am."). As discussed earlier, she did not much care for her program ("It sucks. A full waste of my time."). Instead, most teaching ideas, lesson plans, and pedagogical models came from other teachers at the school—sometimes English department colleagues and sometimes her four social studies friends. When I asked Kim about terminology she used (e.g., *thematic motifs*), she reported learning it from a colleague. When I probed for sources of specific lesson ideas (like "fishbowl" activities or book notes, worksheets, and assessment projects) she referenced her social studies colleagues/friends.

One classroom episode stands out as reflecting the extent to which Kim's personality and personal causes guided her conceptions of teaching and learning. Kim asked her tenth grade students to read a newspaper op-ed piece she had photocopied. The author argued against bestowing honor on "America's founders" (George Washington, Benjamin Franklin, Thomas Jefferson, Patrick Henry, and Abraham Lincoln), because all had held slaves or condoned slavery. (This curricular focus on morality links back to Kim's conceptions of the subject.) During the subsequent class discussion about racism, Kim's strong belief in individual agency became apparent: She believed a person chooses to be racist or not—any structural or historical influences can be rejected if an individual so wishes, and so antiracism is a static choice, not a developmental process. Kim's role as facilitator of the class discussion seemed to be guided by her moral fairness life theme. Students whose comments matched her beliefs received reactions like "Good" or a nod of Kim's head. Comments to the contrary were either met with a "Let me play devil's advocate" follow-up question or received no reaction from Kim at all—she just pointed to the next person with a raised hand. At one point a student named Mark said that Oskar Schindler had treated his employees like slaves, yet, Mark reasoned, "You wanted us to honor him. What's up with that?" At this, Kim abruptly ended the discussion, moving to a conversation about whether it was appropriate for Senator John McCain to have used the word *Gooks* recently to refer to the Vietnamese. When Mark then defended McCain (he lived through it; his hate is justified; he can use any word he wants), Kim became visibly angry and told him he had lost the right to speak, explaining, "It's hard for you [to understand this issue] because you're a white male." At this, another student—named Rob—spoke up and said to Kim: "I think you're putting too much of your personal thoughts into this discussion." Mark applauded and said, "I couldn't agree with you more, Rob." Kim suddenly shut down the class by saying, "Put the desks back; it's time to go; the bell is about to ring." After class, she confronted Rob and told him, "I wholeheartedly disagree with what you said. If you only knew what I wanted to say. I just totally disagree. I'll leave it at that." It had been an unpleasant scene, and it seemed that all students recognized, if they had not already, that to disagree with Kim was to risk immediate (and public) censure and perhaps lasting repercussions. Sure enough, Kim said to me after class, "That kid [Mark] is a bastard. I wish I could have told him to shut the fuck up."

Kim's Teaching Colleagues and Her Credentialing Program

Kim's program influenced only one strand of her pedagogical knowledge (I will discuss it in what follows). Instead, her primary teaching influence was her school colleagues. She rejected learning from program peers ("They're all inexperienced people. They're just as lost as I am."). As discussed earlier, she did not much care for her program. But about her colleagues she frequently told me things like this:

My program taught me nothing. Everything I've gotten has been either
from the teachers at the school or the Internet.
[My colleagues] save me on a daily basis.
The things that taught me how to be a good teacher are the teachers
that I work with.

Sometimes she employed didactic teaching methods—lecturing,
assigning worksheets, having students write short essays or complete short-answer tests. Sometimes she used cooperative learning
techniques—fishbowls, class discussions, group projects. Yet, rather
than consciously assemble a balance out of both teacher-centered and
student-centered instruction approaches, Kim's approach was to lean
on the knowledge sources closest at hand and retain what seemed to
succeed in the classroom.[4] Most teaching ideas and lesson plans came
from other teachers at the school—sometimes English department
colleagues and sometimes her four social studies friends. For her
Community College English (CCE) classes, she told me she sometimes
downloaded lesson plans from teacher Web sites like *OuttaRay'sHead.
com* or—as mentioned previously—planned for her students what she
wished her teachers had done for her. With these twelfth graders, she
eschewed the lesson ideas from her department colleagues (even those
who taught CCE English) as boring and too academically rigorous.
Primarily, her teaching ideas came from her social studies colleagues/
friends:

> I learn by copying. Copying what other teachers are doing.... That
> Holocaust thing. That's a social studies piece. I got it from [my teacher
> friends]. When I did *All Quiet on the Western Front*, I did it because they
> were doing World War I and I got a lot of the material from them. The
> Great Depression stuff. The Rwanda video. And the questions [about
> the Rwanda video] that we're going to do as groups—I got them from
> [the social studies teachers]. I've gotten massive ideas from them, a lot
> of ideas. We talk all the time.

The following interview exchange—as she articulates and defends her
teaching—reveals just how definitively Kim assembled her teaching
philosophy out of personal views and influences. Notice how her explanation of teaching invokes, in order, the following educational beliefs:
(1) Life lessons and functional fluency constitute English curriculum,

(2) her teacher friends are her primary knowledge suppliers, (3) teaching morality is indispensable, and (4) teachers are bound by their own comfort level:

> BRAD: Let's pretend that a parent calls you up and asks you to justify how all this social science–type stuff makes sense in an English classroom. How would you respond?

> KIM: I would answer by saying, "Well, I think that the civil rights movement, the Great Depression, racism, wars are things that should come up in any classroom. It's not strictly an English subject, it's a human subject that I think deserves to be talked about and dealt with in every class. And I want my students to be able to write and read real life situations that our country has gone through, is going through. Be able to articulate their feelings, beliefs, and concerns on it.

> BRAD: Let's say this parent says, "Well, I want them learning about language and literature and how authors affect readers through the language they use. And I want my child to learn how sentences are constructed, and how to write essays, and how her writing can improve. The lessons about racism and the Depression will come up later in his life, or in humanities classes. I'd rather you teach her how to read and write."

> KIM: "Well, sir. Mr. Dad" [laughs], I would say that in order for them to read a book, there are themes about family, survival, race that—if I don't give my kids some sort of background on—they're going to start reading that book, and it's almost like sending them into it blind.... There's so many questions that are going to come up about life, and it would be ridiculous for me not to touch upon these subjects before the questions start coming up. I'd like to have control over it, I guess, instead of them starting to read the book and then going outside and getting into a fight about racism—a white student and a black student. I would rather do it in here, in a structured setting.

> BRAD: But the pre-reading exercises could just as much revolve around literary elements as social elements. These are also things that are going to come up in a piece of literature and will need to be understood in order to make sense of the book. So maybe the question is, Why have you chosen the social angle rather than the literary angle?

> KIM: Because that's the stuff I got from the other teachers. [And] because I'm more comfortable with that stuff. Remember, you teach what you're comfortable with.

Kim's interactional style in the classroom derived from her personal disposition. Much of this was discussed in the previous section, as I wrote about Kim's use of humor, personality, performance, and shared identity with her CCE students, and her less personal, more formalized style with her tenth grade students. An additional dimension is her conception of the power hierarchy in the classroom. Unlike William or Azar, Kim required that students respect the traditional student-teacher hierarchy: Teacher possesses the power, students must unquestioningly obey the teacher's rules. In this regard, there was a confirmatory relationship between her and her program: Each adhered to a rather traditional, behavioristic approach to classroom discipline.[5]

Kim was predisposed to accept her program's traditional approach to discipline because (1) her incoming disposition appeared to have been steeped in a lifetime of behaviorism; (2) order and power in the classroom could have eased her feelings of professional insecurity; (3) she was never exposed to alternative ways of thinking, like postmodern treatments of power (Foucault 1977), constructivist views of discipline (McDaniel 1986), or critical theories of schooling (Freire 1970; Giroux 1992; Gore 1998; Willis 1981); and (4) her own teacher personality closely matched that of her classroom management instructor. These characteristics of her prior experience—contributing to her life themes—engendered an incoming disposition that included a more or less tacit acceptance of traditional classroom discipline common in the high school where she worked and endorsed by her program.[6]

Her program prescribed its approach in a course called classroom management (and inscribed it in the ways Kim interpreted various program politics). Classroom Management was a fall course taught by a veteran high school teacher with an acting/theater background. The instructor designed the curriculum around a video series called *Positive Classroom Management* (Jones 1987), which advocates a step-by-step, prescriptive approach to discipline, and she championed the virtues of the fun, boisterous leader who maintains tight control over students. I observed one lesson where the fifty intern teachers spent forty-one minutes practicing the "teacher stare" ("Terminate instruction. Square those hips toward the student. Drop your jaw so you can get a finger between your teeth, just a pinkie. No, that face looks scared—open your lips. Look not into their eyes but at the bridge of their nose; that way you won't make the direct eye contact that may make you laugh."). And this instructor had students face off against her in a game of Make-Me-Laugh. As she taught, she told jokes, whirled around the room, used comical voices, and referenced hypothetical students like "Bozo Bonnie." Kim later reported that this instructor was "one of only two teachers" at Gould University to whom she ever paid attention. Kim was disposed to accept a powerful performer who entertained students and preached vibrant (if traditional) ways to control kids, and therefore Kim responded confirmatorily to this part of the programmatic experience.

William

As I have mentioned, William entered his credentialing program with a belief that the best learning occurs when students make meaning for themselves. His program offered a constructivist view of teaching and learning that matched his incoming disposition and thus a strong, immediate confirmation took place. He quickly adopted the formalized language of constructivism and cooperative learning. Unlike Azar, William's notions of constructivism were not overtly political. He wanted to encourage students to read, write, and think for themselves, in order to prepare for college and to develop their own identities. Though he papered his walls with political posters and spoke out on some controversial issues that emerged (sexism and hate speech in the classroom, political issues in the community), his primary intent appeared to be preparing students for academic or employment success after graduation and encouraging students to feel comfortable in school. His initial desire to raise issues surrounding race, class, culture, and gender vanished.

William never lectured. He began most classes with a quick-write and then stood in front to talk with students for a while. He would say hello, share announcements, talk about the work for the day or the week. And then he would introduce or review a topic by facilitating a short discussion before giving instructions for a partner or small-group activity. The remainder of the lesson would be spent with students working (or not working) while William circulated—assisting groups and individual students. At the end of the class, William would sometimes host a short closing discussion, often focused on logistics of the work that remained. Designing and implementing lessons, William consciously attempted to integrate programmatic knowledge with his own goals for students.

His interactional style seemed a self-conscious blend of teacher-as-hip-friend and teacher-as-authority (not an uncommon stance for beginning teachers; consider Liz from chapter two). He wanted students to accept and connect with him, but he simultaneously believed that he was unlike them and that these kids required a disciplinarian. Yet he struggled with both parts. Because both ingredients were noticeably *goals* rather than dispositional characteristics or parts of his worldview—because he had not yet taken ownership of them—they seemed a bit wooden and artificial; as a result, students did not always accept the combination; it appeared to me that they did not quite accept that his teacher self was authentic. One teaching model that William never employed was teacher-as-expert; instead, he always gave the impression that any opinion supported by evidence or logic was admissible or at least discussible. He truly believed his knowledge was not superior to his students'—that real learning is constructed, not acquired.

William entered his credentialing program with a belief, stemming from his outdoor education experiences, that the best learning occurs when students discover for themselves. His program offered a constructivist view of teaching and learning that closely matched his incoming disposition, and thus a strong, immediate confirmation took place. He quickly adopted the formalized language of constructivism and cooperative learning.

Liz

Since most of the last chapter was devoted to Liz's conceptions of teaching and learning and her credentialing relationship in that regard, here I will only very briefly summarize Liz's experience. Liz's experience was characterized by a (mostly binary) conflict between her traditional, didactic incoming model of teaching and the progressivist, cooperative one her program advocated. Her teacher knowledge construction was largely a two-year negotiation among, and reconciliation of, opposing models of teaching. Ultimately, she extracted parts of several approaches and assembled them into a personalized hybrid she believed would serve her teaching purposes, her teacher knowledge conceptions, her classroom realities, and her program's urgings. However, she constructed this assemblage without much support from her program because it did not acknowledge the legitimacy of preserving any part of her didactic conception of teaching; this left Liz with an unfavorable view of her program and programmatic experience, and a tentative knowledge hybrid ill suited for her beginning experiences in the classroom.

As previously mentioned, Liz's experience was characterized by a binary conflict between her traditional, didactic incoming model of pedagogy and the progressivist, cooperative one her program advocated. Her teacher identity development was largely a two-year negotiation between, and reconciliation of, opposing models of teaching: her father's traditional model of expert delivering content versus her program's student-centered model of students teaching themselves in groups. Ultimately, she extracted parts of both approaches and assembled them into a fragile hybrid she believed would serve her teaching purposes, her teacher knowledge conceptions, her classroom realities, and her program's urgings. However, Liz believed this blend did not succeed in the classroom, and by the time year two ended, she had become despondent and bitter about both teaching and her credentialing program.

Common Themes Across All Four Teachers

Already, these four beginning teachers demonstrate a range of knowledge, effectiveness, instructional approaches, and types of student with whom they are most comfortable. Yet a few commonalities merit mention. One commonality is that all four experienced crises of authority. Azar experienced an authority bind in relation to her immigrant status. Kim underwent problematic relationships to her leadership authority with students whose opinions she did not share and to her academic authority with what she perceived as intimidating subject expectations held by her honors students. William's problems with classroom authority resulted from his viewing students as so different from him that he had trouble creating a balanced stance between dual continua of distance and intimacy, leader and friend. And Liz faced difficulty releasing her (traditional, didactic) teacher authority as she attempted to embrace a more student-centered teaching model. These crises of authority are not new (Bird et al. 1993; Fuller and Bown 1975; Weinstein 1990), but, as this study illustrates, their sources and ways of forming are explainable. The contours and consequences of each teacher's authority bind can be located inside the conflict between one's life themes/incoming dispositions and the reality shock of teaching. For the novice teacher struggling to develop a professional identity that balances one's own self, one's professional goals, the approaches of the preparation program, and the many demands of the classroom, how to position oneself in relation to power, authority, and a desire to encourage authentic student learning becomes terribly complicated. Because these four teacher education programs mostly avoided explicit conversations about how to do this, the teachers were left to their own devices. This meant that Kim, Liz, and Azar might have overprivileged their own default conceptions (their personal identities), and William might have underprivileged his. In all cases, the results—at least during this point in their developing careers—were awkward, tentative, and not necessarily successful.

A second commonality is that all four teachers had various kinds of trouble relating to students who were not like themselves. Again, this is not an uncommon finding (Avery and Walker 1993; Barry and Lechner 1995; Delpit 1995; Quiocho and Ross 2000; Tatum 1999) but one whose embedded processes this study has sought to analyze. If the process of constructing knowledge is directed by prior constructs, then conservative pulls of familiar knowledge and self-reinforcing subjectivism will inevitably privilege prior conceptions over new knowledge models. This accounts for Azar neglecting to consider alternative relationships to her immigrant stance and failing to reflect critically on her incoming teaching disposition. It explains why Kim felt at ease with the twelfth graders but antagonistic toward the tenth graders, and explains her commitment to viewing teaching through the lens of her own schooling experiences. It allows us to better understand ways in which William's strongly confirmatory program experience around African-American students as objects of study, though for admirable reasons, encouraged him in some ways to pathologize his students' culture(s). And it assists in understanding Liz's reality shock and her decision to lower expectations. Only when these topics are raised explicitly for beginning teachers and addressed openly (and honestly) in professional settings will novices begin to acknowledge the power their pasts have on their views of students, race, class, gender, and sexual orientation. This kind of cultural identity work, artfully conducted, can encourage teachers to become more aware, and in more control, of relying on their personal identities as they construct their professional ones.

Third, the credentialing programs—to various extents—did not impel teacher candidates to confront and/or problematize their incoming conceptions about teaching and learning. Azar's program was fairly well positioned to engage Azar in the consideration of alternative ideas about teaching and learning, and to an extent this occurred. But in areas of subject knowledge, teaching as a political act, and her own biographical biases, the program was mostly silent; this silence allowed Azar's prior beliefs to go unchallenged. William's credentialing relationship was so strongly confirmatory that much of his incoming disposition was instantly legitimized—this shut down critical self-reflection, what Sharon Feiman-Nemser and Margret Buchmann (1985) refer to as the "familiarity pitfall." But I do not believe this is entirely distressing: It might also be evidence that William had done substantive reflection before matriculating and already held well-examined beliefs upon which his program could build (Bird et al. 1993; Levin and Ammon 1992). Nevertheless, his ways of relating to students might have been smoother and therefore more effective if his developing identity had included deeper attention to alternative ways of viewing urban students of color and his own pedagogical relationship to these students. Kim's overreliance on her affective stance toward credentialing, in general, and her program instructors, specifically, proved considerable. She entered her program disposed to reject it, quickly disengaging when the program conceptions did not resemble her prior ideas and/or the instructors were unlikable. This meant that for Kim, her programmatic experience in no way altered or further developed her knowledge. In terms of her identity development, it seemed only to deepen her animosity toward official schooling, certain kinds of educators, and teacher education in general. Liz's program was not positioned to help her relinquish her prior beliefs and, furthermore, the interpersonal dynamics between her and two of her professors facilitated rejection of their knowledge. In all cases, it was the complex process of interrelation among experiences, dispositions, and knowledge sources—not some direct acquisition of programmatic knowledge—that embodied the teachers' professional learning.

Program Positionings

Each teacher's life experiences produced a particular set of incoming conceptions and dispositions about teaching, learning, subject, and schooling that positioned the teacher in identifiable ways inside his or her credentialing program. This positioning—along with the personal relationships formed—largely accounted for the specific credentialing experience each candidate had. The previous sections, while deconstructing and investigating the development of each candidate's professional knowledge, also offered micro-examinations of the relationship between person and program. This section provides a more macroscopic look at those relationships. There are two sets of (themselves interrelating) variables that interacted to create each candidate's experience. One is the set of conceptions, dispositions, and reasons for teaching held by the matriculating student; the other is the set of knowledges, values, and philosophies put forward by the credentialing program. Each teacher's credentialing experience existed inside the relationship between the two sets of characteristics. Figure 3.2 represents those relationships.

William's incoming sociopolitical view of schooling, his constructivist (before he knew the word) understanding of learning, and his strong subject background were well matched with his program's acceptance of both academic and social justice teaching goals, privileging constructivist views of learning and singular emphasis on the teaching of English/ESL. This explains his confirmatory relationship with the program and his personally pleasant experience at Frederic University. Yet it also illustrates a pitfall of confirmatory experiences: His program was rarely positioned to confront him with his own knowledge limitations and biases. There were places for him to interrogate his own assumptions (a standard tenet of sociocultural perspectives like his program's), but because his prior understandings matched his program's they were tacitly encouraged.

Liz's preparation program strongly rejected her father's traditional, product approach to English teaching in favor of student-centered, cooperative learning, process approaches. This conflict presented Liz with a discord that required her to evaluate both models and reconcile opposites. Because she was engaged in learning-to-teach and her program, she accepted the challenge. Because she experienced some unpleasant interpersonal dynamics with her two primary professors, and because she had already seen her father's model succeed, she was more willing to reject her program than her incoming conceptions. Over time, she fashioned a kind of mixture that incorporated pieces of each paradigm, but this compromise was fragile and had not coalesced into something that satisfied her professional and personal teacher needs. Her program, therefore, was positioned to encourage Liz to confront her prior conceptions and grapple with their consequences for her own teaching goals, though in its inability to provide a comfortable space—a scaffold of sorts—for Liz to evaluate her prior understandings without fully rejecting them, it inadvertently nudged her toward rejection of much of her program. This demonstrates that not only must a program invite students into knowledge and identity conflicts, it must also understand

(C = Confirmatory
D = Disconfirmatory
A = Appropriating)

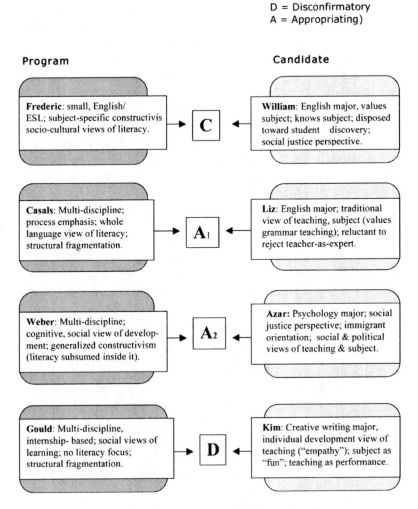

Figure 3.2   The Programs and the Candidates

the subtle contours of those conflicts and be prepared to assist students to *find their way out* of the conflicts safely and smartly.

Azar entered her program on the heels of a powerful and rewarding undergraduate experience that had politically radicalized her and deepened her belief that social psychology is the most effective lens through which to view education. She matriculated in a program that subordinated political views of learning, teaching, and schooling under social and academic versions of student development, and a program that did not always distinguish between the teaching of English and the other secondary education disciplines. Azar chose to meaningfully engage in her program studies partly because the program's reputation was high, partly because she liked and respected the faculty, and partly because she had always enjoyed school and academics. Yet she was quick to find fault. She rejected her program's neglect of political activism, rejected its focus on the school and classroom (instead of the larger community) as the primary unit of analysis, and rejected its emphasis on cognitive and academic dimensions of learning over political ones. Within these conflicts she confidently retained her prior understandings and unproblematically dismissed her program as mostly "not for me." But she did believe that her program could provide specific teaching strategies. She embraced the program's student-centered teaching methods, cooperative learning approaches, and other progressivist techniques, using them as means to achieve her incoming ends for teaching. Also, because this program rarely addressed subject knowledge, it was unable to uncover Azar's rather rudimentary understandings of English language and literature and her tendency to substitute for that lack with reader response activities focused on "how did the text make you feel?" and open-ended discussions about politics, identity, and student lives outside school.

Kim entered her program predisposed to reject it. She had taught for one year as a long-term substitute and believed she already understood teaching; she unproblematically trusted her own high school memories as knowledge source; her school colleagues had shared their own unflattering portraits of the credentialing experience; she had never been entirely comfortable with academic learning—or "book smarts" as she called it—and believed most educators made school boring. Her program unwittingly played into these predispositions. Kim perceived her cohort director as mean, hypocritical, and insulting, and this cohort director spent a lot of time with Kim: She taught a summer course, coordinated the internships, and met regularly with the candidates. The program put forward a (structurally fragmented) professional approach that, to Kim, resembled the boring academic learning she hated—instructors lecturing, students seated in desks taking notes, reading textbooks, and taking tests. This meant that even though there was the potential for confirmatory experiences (Kim and her program both viewed teacher education pragmatically, valued concrete methods over abstract theorizing, and applied behaviorist perspectives to teaching and learning), it went unrealized because her program did not present itself in ways that invited Kim to enter into and engage with it. I do not believe Kim would have rejected *any* credentialing program; I think that the particular personal-professional dynamics set by the cohort director and the institutionalized "look" of traditional schooling this program put forth largely explain Kim's immediate disengagement.

This entire chapter—especially this concluding discussion of the kinds of relationships that exist between person and program—suggests that teacher preparation programs can benefit from increased attention to the prior and personal dimensions of teacher candidates. If programs make visible the embedded ways beginning teachers automatically rely on their prior experiences to construct professional knowledge, they can interrupt the process. If done with care and respect, teacher education can become the meaningful professional intervention it seeks to be. The following—and concluding—chapter offers a set of discussions designed to recommend how programs can better embrace these holistic, iterative, situated processes of teacher identity development.

Notes

1. C. G. Jung might call it an individual's *Weltanschauung,* or "philosophy of life" (Jung 1970).

2. For example, resistance theories (e.g., Kohl 1991; Willis 1981) or cultural incompatibility models (e.g., Ogbu 1990a, 1990b) argue that members of disenfranchised populations sometimes actively resist the acculturation—or submission—they perceive successful mainstream schooling constitutes. Azar unproblematically presumed that, because immigration and a commitment to U.S. schooling had been good for her and her family, they would be good for any immigrant.

3. This taps into a crucial domain of multicultural education that examines ways white teachers construct their own identities and those of their students with regard to race, ethnicity, class, and language. See Banks 2002; Foster 1998; Grant and Sleeter 2006; McIntosh 1988; Tatum 1999.

4. And what "succeeded" was typically evaluated through the lens of her own life themes. This meant that performance satisfaction, the appearance of student engagement, students discussing moral issues, and a minimum of teacher work were the primary criteria.

5. By "traditional approach," I mean a prescriptive model of classroom discipline descending from the middle-twentieth-century era of large schools, centralized authority, standardized notions of students (and behavior), and behavioristic theories of human development. Underlying premises include these: Instruction and discipline are separate entities, discipline precedes instruction, learning requires order, students should (and can) always follow the teacher's direction, and punishment works (McDaniel 1986; Powell et al. 2001).

6. Kim rejected her high school teachers' instructional approaches as boring, but appeared never to have isolated or problematized their discipline approaches. It seems that she never considered there could be an alternative way to envision and approach behavior and power relations in the classroom. I suspect this results from the first three of the four factors mentioned in the text.

4

Conclusions and Implications
for Practice and Research
in Teacher Education

A prejudice is a principle its owner does not intend to examine.
—*Wallace Stegner*

The question my study set out to answer was, *How and from where does a beginning teacher's knowledge emerge?* Considering it further, I had developed several subquestions:

- What are the influences on learning-to-teach; how do they interrelate? Are there similar processes across the teachers? What accounts for the differences?
- What roles does context play in knowledge construction?
- What are reasons why—and conditions under which—influences and contexts trigger or mute, fit or oppose, or in some way affect the effects of each other? Where is this common across participants?
- What makes certain experiences confirmatory, other ones disconfirmatory, and still others interacting without directly conflicting?

I have concluded that learning to teach is not the mostly direct, linear, hyperrational, mental process that is often presumed. Instead, I found teachers developing through the holistic, recursive process I have described throughout this book: Past, present, and future interrelate in tangled ways as an individual continually reassembles understandings in relation to perceived contexts with direct and indirect help from multiple influences and social relationships. In other words, an adult learner draws on past experiences via personal constructs that organize understanding and assemble conceptions considered aligned with both past positionings and present context in order to navigate the future. (Say that three times fast!) The adult learner seeks a kind of epistemological balance, or coherence, from the negotiation among often-conflicting sources of knowledge. This perceived knowledge-and-identity balance allows the developing teacher, consciously or not, to believe his or her professional self is reasonable. If there's imbalance—some kind of knowledge dissonance—the teacher concludes something is wrong and works (again, consciously or not) to solve the dissonance by rejecting, adjusting, or reframing knowledge strands in regard to one's prior self. In light of this teacher learning process, distinctions between personal and professional become moot. Boundaries between affect and intellect blur. Experience and thought conflate. Subjectivism and objectivism collapse into phenomenology.

Explicit conversations with pre-service and in-service teachers, formalized teacher identity curricula, and an emphasis on encouraging teachers to take conscious ownership of their professional identities will help teachers better direct their own professional learning. This should allow them to delimit the undesirable results of this process and foreground the useful ones. As teachers, teacher educators, and professional development specialists grapple with refining and improving their practice, this study raises several findings that merit consideration. This final chapter is organized first to review some key themes that emerged, second to revisit useful notions of teacher learning, and third to offer some suggestions for practice. Guiding them is the primary argument that teacher education, in both theory and practice, should make visible this embedded teacher knowledge-and-identity development process.

Learning Was Both Individual and Social, Both Cognitive and Situated

Each teacher created understandings, skills, and dispositions while reflecting alone; interacting with others; and relying on subjective memories and interpretations of context, social events, and practices. In other words, professional learning included both social processes and individual ones. For example, in chapter two I discussed Liz learning to distinguish among and evaluate teaching models. She was automatically structuring her thinking by considering multiple influences: her father, her own schooling experiences, her girlfriend, ideology, worldview, her education professors, assigned texts, and credentialing contexts. These influences were themselves organized by dispositional guides like her personality, a lifetime of cultural positionings, and contemporary *episteme* characteristics. That all these influences exist seems an important acknowledgment. Moreover, that each influence mediates (and is mediated by) all the others in identifiable ways to construct knowledge seems both exciting and powerful.

To accept this process requires accepting both individual theories of learning and social ones. Liz used her father's influence in relation to her high school memories, her experiences with English, and her teaching goals to interpret texts and teachers who both taught her and emotionally affected her, while she was simultaneously discussing education with her girlfriend, her family, and me, furthermore interacting with high school teachers, students, and program peers most every day in ways emotional, intellectual, academic, political, and creative inside multiple contexts shaped by multiple institutional and social practices. That is nineteen influences (and only a partial list). The wider we cast the research net, the more influences on teacher learning we capture. However, it was Liz as a distinctive self (existing inside autobiographical space and time) who developed and enacted the products of these understandings. Another person in the same learning environment would have constructed and enacted knowledge differently. This kind of framing allows for a consideration of the individual as having a singular experience, but one to be understood as inextricably joined to the multiple social contexts in which he or she participates (Bakhtin in Holquist 1990; Holland et al. 1998; G. H. Mead 1964/1932; Vygotsky 1978). This leads to a shift away from the discrete "teacher knowledge" as unit of analysis toward a broader, more situated, recursive notion signaled by "teacher identity" instead. Teacher identity as unit of analysis widens and deepens how we can examine and understand influences on teacher development.

Teacher Knowledge Development
Was Both Chronological and Iterative

Two processes of knowledge development occurred simultaneously within each teacher's experience. There was development over time—a forward-moving notion that sits at the center of most constructivist theories of teacher development (Fosnot 1996; Levin and Ammon 1992; Piaget 1972): Liz, for example, entered her credentialing program with a set of understandings, conceptions, and beliefs about teaching that expanded and changed during the two years in response to intended and unintended interventions. At the end of our time together, she exited with a different set of understandings, conceptions, and beliefs. Yet that macroscopic chronological conception of development consists, in fact, of an embedded series of microscopic processes that constitute how a person's understandings and dispositions change. This set of micro-processes is the knowledge process, and it is not linear. For example, chapter two illustrates that, while Liz traveled through our two years together, she was constructing knowledge in an iterative fashion. Described by the cut-and-paste metaphor from chapter one, she was processing new stimuli by combining them with, and testing them against, various prior conceptions and sources. For example, she drew on her own memories of her life and what she believed those have taught her as she interpreted and constructed meaning from her many teacher education experiences. This more micro-minded process is tangled and circular. That a chronological process of teacher development occurred along with this recursive knowledge process evokes an image of them existing on top of each other, like the representation in Figure 4.1.

The knowledge process circles around and around, constructing knowledge continuously out of available materials past and present, while the chronological teacher education experience moves Liz forward; the result is a sequenced path of circles—a forward-moving spiral.

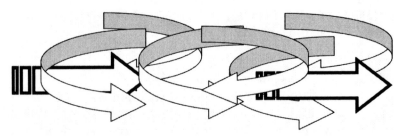

Figure 4.1   Macro- and Micro-Processes of Knowledge Construction

There Existed a Tendency Toward Knowledge Balance, or Knowledge Coherence

In chapter two I wrote that as Liz naturally (and automatically) strove for coherence in assembling her teacher knowledge, she was manipulating, juxtaposing, and fastening bundles of professional and personal interpretations, identities, memories, and ways of knowing into something she considered (consciously or not) coherent. I pointed to multiple traditions of inquiry articulating this point: Eastern religion, hermeneutics, psychoanalysis, and social psychology all posit versions of an inherent human tendency toward balance. Liz's story was often about her attempt to reconcile knowledge sources that appeared to her incongruous—to solve the cognitive dissonance she believed she was experiencing. Likewise, Azar, William, and Kimberly experienced a tacit push to assemble their professional identity such that a kind of harmony formed. This harmony, it was presumed, would produce a comfort that, in turn, would confirm that a professional self had been—or was being—successfully assembled.[1]

But where does this tendency toward balance come from? I do not know, although I can posit three guesses. Perhaps it is the result of research bias—an inherent desire on the part of researchers like myself to achieve a symmetry of findings, to have all the loose ends tie up neatly. Or, perhaps it is a product of our *episteme*: that in this modern (or late modern or postmodern) age, we have accepted as a priori truth the existence and desirability of an omnipotent, omnipresent harmony to which all things adhere, and in positing this we have, in fact, created it. These first two possibilities certainly join up and link to postmodern claims about coherence as an artificial construct (Foucault 1970, 1977; Lemert 1997; Lyotard 1984/1979). Or, maybe balance is actually a cosmic state. This is my third guess. Maybe harmony is, in fact, one of those underlying principles of the universe and, because humans participate in and originate from the universe's energy, they, too, are governed by its laws (consider string theory physics [Greene 1999]). This remains one of those open questions that guides inquiry and gives rise to ongoing philosophical debate. Whichever the cause, the effects should not be neglected by teacher education. Teacher educators who ignore beginning teachers' strong need to feel some kind of identity balance in the midst of what is usually an extremely unbalanced entry into the teaching profession do so at their own peril.

The Personal Was Often Stronger Than the Programmatic

When Azar confronted a credentialing program that privileged academic learning and cognitive constructivism over more politicized views of adolescent development, she unquestioningly chose her own, critical theory views over Weber's more academic, developmentalist ones. She mostly liked her program, and she embraced its teaching methods, but appropriated them to fit her own goals and conceptions. Whenever Kim found her program advocating purely academic treatments of teaching and learning, she remembered her own unhappy schooling experiences, applied them to her conceptions of students, and concluded that her program was wrong and her intuition right. She followed her own "commonsense" understandings (or folk theories: Feiman-Nemser and Buchmann 1986), and merely feigned learning from her program. William's credentialing experience was confirmatory (and therefore pleasant for him) because the programmatic mostly confirmed the personal. As Liz faced a conflict between her father's traditional, grammar-heavy, pedagogical content knowledge and her program's cooperative, process-based knowledge, she instinctively assigned higher values to what came from her father. It became clear that within knowledge conflicts, the personal typically trumped the programmatic. This echoes Bird et al. (1993), finding prospective teachers' prior beliefs strongly resilient against alternative beliefs, and these teachers reluctant to consider teaching and learning models different from those coming from their own personal experience. It also offers a new interpretation of Kenneth Zeichner and Robert Tabachnick (1981) finding programmatic conceptions "washed out" from the active knowledge of newly prepared teachers: Perhaps new teachers, as they fit it to themselves, bend their programs' knowledge to such an extent that it becomes unrecognizable by its original owners.

This facet of teacher learning proves both the challenge and the hope inside pre-service professional development. The challenge is to accept pre-service teacher education as a short-term intervention in a decades-long process of socialization, acculturation, and formative learning (Rust 1994). Instead, we should view learning-to-teach as a career-long process and one in which continuous hybridization might be the more realistic goal, not sudden transformation.[2] However, there are opportunities, too. One is that, because this embedded process of knowledge construction appears to be mostly unconscious, the act of making it conscious can offer learners significantly more control over their learning. Teacher educators who encourage pre-service teachers to become aware of their own learning processes—to identify individualized knowledge sources and ways they interrelate—will better position students to themselves delimit unwanted knowledge and promote desirable knowledge. "If we can recognize the shackles tradition has placed on us," writes Franz Boas, "we are also able to break them" (quoted in Fairclough 1989).

The second opportunity is that knowing is dynamic, not static, and results from interaction among many variables. Engaged teachers are forever learning and finding new ways to conceive of their practice and themselves as professionals. There is always potential for development, incremental though it might be. And because knowledge derives from interrelation among many factors, an individual can control some variables even if others remain uncontrollable. A teacher is influenced by his or her past but never wholly bound to it; it exists as only part of a fluid knowledge equation. This interactionist view of development—individual and culture interact to jointly produce a self (G. H. Mead 1964/1932; Rosaldo 1989; Woods 1996)—provides a kind of Houdini-like escape maneuver from the straightjacket of structural determinism.

Subject Knowledge Structured Learning-to-Teach

Liz and William both entered their programs with strong disciplinary backgrounds in English. For Liz's experience, this meant both that her English focus seemed to her to be more important than it did to her program and that her particular teaching experience was dominated by attempts to instill within students the same respect for, commitment to, and expertise in language and literature she had learned. As chapter two explains, both aspects caused her trouble. In William's case the strong subject background meant that his program could build off his disciplinary knowledge to better help him recast his English student experiences into English teacher experiences. He appreciated this, and it contributed to his confirmatory program experience. Conversely, both Azar and Kimberly matriculated with relatively weak subject matter backgrounds. This meant four things. It meant that they compensated for disciplinary weaknesses with a reflexive reliance on what they did know—life lessons, political critiques, and morality instruction. It meant that they conceived of their subject as something they would learn over time by reflecting on their teaching. It meant in Kim's case that she experienced some anxiety and professional insecurity when teaching honors students. And it meant that when both their programs presumed candidates possessed a strong subject expertise from which they could build, they presumed falsely. The programs were unable to unearth Azar's and Kim's weak disciplinary background, because neither program expected it to exist.

William's program was the only one devoted solely to teachers of English/English language learners (ELL), and I found this a mostly beneficial characteristic: As mentioned in chapter three, it meant that most peer talk and programmatic lessons focused on the teaching of English, and therefore candidates had substantial scaffolding in the teaching of their subject area. It also, though, created a sacrifice: William reported receiving neither familiarity with cross-disciplinary approaches to instruction nor any formalized attention to interdisciplinary teaching.

Personal Dimensions of Professional Relationships Mattered

Any relationship, even a professional one, is influenced by multiple dimensions of affect. Power relations (Foucault 1977); issues of face-saving (Goffman 1959; Gumperz 1982), status, and social capital (Bourdieu 1991; de Certeau 1984) and the centrality of emotions (Goleman 1996) shape the nature of any interaction between people. This means that the professional consequences of any professional relationship derive from personal-emotional contours as much as from professional-intellectual ones. This has been examined within teachers' collegial relations (Kelchtermans 1996; Little 1990; Olsen and Kirtman 2002; Sisken 1994), and I found it true for relationships between credentialing students and their instructors. Chapter two presented ways in which Liz's negative feelings toward her methods professor (feelings of defensiveness/insecurity, of antipathy) facilitated a rejection of the professor's knowledge and, conversely, ways in which Liz's positive feelings toward her reading professor (feelings of respect and appreciation) encouraged acceptance of this professor's knowledge. In chapter three, Kim explained her rejection of the Gould program as resulting directly from the immediate hostility she felt toward the cohort leader and, simultaneously, reported heeding her classroom management instructor's knowledge because "I like her." This means that those teacher educators who create a personal dynamic that offers (at least the appearance of) comfort, security, and an appreciation for the individual learner appear better positioned to meaningfully engage students with the material.

Personality Mattered

I have neither the training nor the desire to delve deeply into a discussion of personality types, traits, and assessment inventories. Truthfully, I am reluctant to talk about personality at all. The embedded effects of armchair psychologizing and social discrimination that have burrowed into the topic (e.g., Gray's [1993] *Men Are from Mars, Women Are from Venus* or Herrnstein and Murray's [1996] *The Bell Curve*, respectively), and extreme forms of postmodernism and political correctness that refuse any claim to objectivity (for critiques, see Giroux 1992 or Leo 2002) have made it difficult to talk about personality. Yet, I did find that what might be better termed "personality dispositions" (Hamachek 1999) or "personality configurations" (Gardner 1993) affected the development of the teachers I studied.[3] I found the following five personal characteristics to be relevant in helping to account for the teachers' knowledge development: (1) reflectiveness/capacity for reflection, (2) confidence, (3) creativity, (4) willingness to experiment, and (5) optimism. I found that each characteristic mediated other influences on learning-to-teach. Below are some of the interrelationships I found.

Degree of reflectiveness affected compatibility with program. For example, William's high capacity for reflection fit with his program's theoretical approach to the study of learning and teaching. This confirmatory relationship facilitated his comfort with the program. *Confidence correlated positively with comfort in teaching role, which, itself, had a positive effect on relationships with students and satisfaction with teaching.* For example, Azar's inherent confidence in herself meant that any professional doubts or insecurity she felt became subordinated under a faith that she would succeed; she was therefore able to experience a high level of comfort in her role as teacher, which, in turn, facilitated student acceptance of her as a legitimate professional. *Willingness to experiment seems to have strengthened teachers' confirmatory relationships with programs.* Frances Fuller and Oliver Bown (1975) first introduced the notion that student teachers (preoccupied with surviving the school day) often resist programmatic inducements to experiment and reflect critically;

others have since examined tensions between teacher educator expectations (experimentation, reflection) and those held by student teachers (survival)—see Marvin Wideen, Jolie Mayer-Smith, and Barbara Moon (1998) for a review. Yet, this paradox diminishes when the student teacher already possesses a willingness to experiment. This was true, for example, in the case of Azar whose willingness to experiment increased the fit between her and the experimentally minded expectations of her program and practicum supervisors.

The sources of an individual's personality configuration remain a mystery to me—some characteristics might derive from early experiences (Freud 1961/1909); others might have been encouraged by current life details, cultural contexts, and personal relationships (Borich 1999; Gardner 1993); surely all result from a complicated interaction among inherited tendencies, sociopolitical landscapes, and lived experiences (Bourdieu 1991; G. H. Mead 1964/1932; Scheibe 1995). Also, I found that each characteristic, itself, affected (i.e., muted or encouraged) the other characteristics; for example, Azar's confidence accentuated her optimism, and both encouraged a willingness to experiment. But, the role of personality in teacher development should be treated carefully. This acknowledgment of personality as performative variable should not, I believe, lead to screening teachers' personalities before employment (e.g., Haberman 1995) or overemphasizing personality, because knowledge—as mentioned earlier—is not static, and personality is only one mediating strand among many active variables. Because it is the interaction that is important, personality should be treated as one determinant of, but not a final conclusion about, any beginning teacher's professional knowledge.

The Credentialing Relationship Between Candidate and Program Determined the Type of Credentialing Experience the Candidate Has

I do not mean that sentence as mere semantics; I mean to imply that the credentialing relationship (confirmatory, disconfirmatory, appropriating) mostly accounted for the nature of the overall credentialing experience. William is described in previous chapters to have had a mostly confirmatory experience; Kim is viewed as having had a mostly disconfirmatory experience. Both Liz's and Azar's experiences were appropriating. I do not wish to imply that a confirmatory experience is necessarily superior; in fact, as discussed in chapter three, William's confirmatory program relationship in some ways precluded him from interrogating his own assumptions, which meant that his credentialing program was not always the socialization *interruption* for which one might hope. But this is not conclusive. As also mentioned, this confirmatory relationship could have derived in part from William having done serious critical reflection—a kind of prior interruption—before he matriculated. This would create a confirmatory relationship resembling one in which biases were allowed to directly pass through the gestalt filter but that, in fact, was the product of two consciously considered, self-reflective approaches to teaching and learning being compatible.

It is my belief that the goal of a teacher education program is not necessarily to produce confirmatory relationships but to ensure that students engage meaningfully with the program material. I do, however, believe that disconfirmatory credentialing relationships are worthless: A novice teacher who entirely rejects her program has wasted significant time and resources—not least among them her own; such a situation describes Kim's credentialing experience. This might be the fault of either the learner or the program, or the product of a fundamental incompatibility between the two.

An ideal programmatic experience—following from the findings of this study—would structure opportunities for students to explicitly interrogate their own assumptions and enter into knowledge conflicts while interacting with programmatic conceptions and alternative beliefs. This would encourage students to confront their life themes, their biases, and their particular ways of organizing phenomena into knowledge to produce the knowledge awareness I described earlier. Significant appropriation would occur, but it would be conscious and would be collaboratively directed by learner, program faculty, and teaching peers working together. Of course, there would need to be enough confirmation to provide students with the confidence required to critically confront one's own biases, but too much confirmation precludes self-critique. Teacher educators who create challenging yet supportive, rigorous yet sympathetic experiences that compel critical reflection in relation to researched knowledge stand a better chance of generating meaningful experiences. Such an approach recognizes both the usefulness of existing theory and the need for learners to actively construct ways of knowing in their field.

And yet, just as importantly, teacher educators have an obligation to help students *extricate* themselves from those knowledge conflicts. A program that invites students into knowledge conflicts without assisting them out risks knowledge rejection. This is because the personal seems to be stronger than the programmatic. A learner can experience cognitive dissonance for only so long; after a while—if there is no reconciliation (what Piaget would call equilibration)—the learner will reject the programmatic in favor of the more deeply embedded personal. This describes aspects of Liz's credentialing experience and parts of Azar's. Teacher educators must find ways to challenge novice teachers' incoming beliefs against alternatives suggested by research, theory, and other learners; and they must assist the novices in reconfiguring their prior knowledge and ways of knowing so that potential dissonance and ambiguities are transcended. I am not quite foolish enough, however, to consider this easy. Tom Bird et al. (1993) have written candidly of the inherent pitfalls (among them the paradox of instructor as simultaneously expert and facilitator, and the discomfort accompanying "ambiguities and risks" [p. 223] of pre-service teacher self-critique). I do believe, though, it is a worthy goal and one that can, in fact, be achieved through attentive and talented teaching, a well-understood programmatic vision, and the necessary institutional and community support.

Considerations for Approaching Practice

This final section exists in two parts. First is a discussion of the kind of knowledge awareness I believe this study calls for: I discuss reflection-in-action, mindfulness, and transformative adult learning in order to offer a new way to think about beginning teachers increasing their knowledge efficacy. Second is a short series of program suggestions teacher educators and researchers might wish to consider as they work to refine teacher preparation.

Reflection-in-Action, Gestalt, and Mindfulness

In the first chapter I wrote about Eastern religion and Buddhist notions of mindfulness in teaching; here is a good place to build on that discussion by raising the need for teacher education to privilege alternative perspectives of reflection, thinking, and acting within teacher learning.

Donald Schön's (1987) "reflection-in-action" collapsed distinctions between theory and practice, between—for example—teacher knowledge and a teacher's knowledge. Whereas many separate theory from practice (e.g., Dewey 1933; Shulman 1987), Schön argues the two often occur together—each informing the other and both becoming intertwined. *Reflection-in-action* is Schön's term for the practice of engaging in a continuous dialogue of reflective inquiry with a situation *while it is occurring*. It nicely connects the thinking part and the acting-in-context part of teacher learning.

Fred Korthagen and Jos Kessels (1999) extend this idea. They credit Schön's advance but have reservations about any linear, hyperrational notion of teacher reflection in which a teacher encounters a situation, interprets it, thinks about it logically, makes a decision, and then acts (e.g., Dewey 1933; Schön 1987). In actuality, the authors argue, an encountered situation triggers a sudden, simultaneous rush of reason, feeling, former experiences, values, role conceptions, needs, images, and routines that consciously and unconsciously guide the teacher's (re)action. All together—irrational responses and rational understandings, thoughts and feelings, memories and predictions—within a split second combine to form the teacher's personal meaning of the situation and, therefore, guide subsequent interpretation and knowledge construction.

Robert Tremmel moves ways of viewing teacher learning even further. Tremmel's "Zen and the Art of Reflective Practice in Teacher Education" (1993) argues that by embracing the Zen Buddhist notion of mindfulness in teacher reflection, we can improve practice. Quoting from Renee Clift and W. Robert Houston, he dismisses the traditional notion of teacher thinking:

> Current definitions of reflection are strongly influenced by the Western cultural heritage, which emphasizes analysis and problem-solving as opposed to negotiation, contemplation, or enlightenment. (p. 434)

"Mindfulness" is focused awareness of the right now and the right here: a space where spirituality, physicality, cognition, and emotions intersect. A space where no divisions exist between knowing and acting, between teacher knowledge and personal ways of being, between past and present, self and other. Mindfulness—the ability to be deeply aware of everything occurring *right now*—looks a bit like Schön's reflection-in-action or Korthagen and Kessels's gestalt but radically broadened and deepened to include the whole experience of being alive. Thich Nhat Hanh, a Vietnamese Zen Buddhist monk, is quoted by Tremmel:

> When walking, the practitioner must be conscious that he is walking. When sitting, the practitioner must be conscious that he is sitting.... Practicing thus, the practitioner lives in direct and constant mindfulness ... we must be conscious of each breath, each movement, every thought and feeling, everything which has any relation to ourselves.

Mindfulness is the term Tremmel uses to effect a total collapsing of all aspects of thinking/acting into one space of enlightened practice.[4]

Though admittedly distant from typically considered Western notions of knowledge, research, and education, his ideas remind us that beyond any set of epistemological blinders we can conceive of, there is still another. We can view Tremmel's mindfulness as attempting to posit a goal where practitioners (in this case, beginning teachers) seize control over their learning by becoming mindful of the many influences on learning and the process of learning so that a kind of "knowledge awareness" increases knowledge autonomy. A teacher who has learned to become fully attentive and sensitive to the classroom as a deep reality without borders is able to perceive not only surface phenomena but also the embedded (and interrelated) impulse and responses of students and teacher existing together to create the space in which they are existing. In this way, a teacher is better positioned to attend to broad and deep conceptions of his or her own identity as influencing the learning, teaching, and/or teacher development that is occurring.

A Transformative Theory of Adult Learning

Jack Mezirow (1991, 2000) articulates a theory of adult learning that explicitly draws on those ideas from Martin Heidegger and George Kelly discussed in chapter one, and implicitly invokes both the knowledge construction process detailed throughout this book and notions of mindfulness just described. Mezirow first distinguishes between child/adolescent learning and adult learning: Child and adolescent learning is *formative* (knowledge is built, understandings form, identities emerge), while adult learning is *transformative* (understandings and identities already formed are reconsidered and reassembled). In other words, a young learner creates knowledge, but an adult learner—already in possession of knowledge—instead reconstructs relationships to existing knowledge, or "reconstrues one's frames of reference" (1991, 4). Like Kelly (1955, 1963), Mezirow locates this interpretive knowledge process inside individual frames of reference derived from a learner's early life experiences. Mezirow then posits two kinds of adult learning: that which occurs automatically and uncritically, and the more desirable type, which occurs through critical reflection as an adult first makes his or her interpretive frames and prior understandings an object of study and then reevaluates and reassembles knowledge to create new knowledge constructs better suited for the present reality. This echoes Paulo Freire's (1970) *conscientization,* or Jean Piaget's (1954, 1972) equilibration made conscious. The solution, as Mezirow explains, is to assist adult learners in the creation of new templates for learning.

Simply put, adult learners need a construct to organize their learning; if they are not offered a new one, they will rely on their prior/personal one(s). Teacher education program personnel should meet to talk openly about the particular underlying frames of teaching, teacher learning, and student learning on which they, themselves, rely. These can be discussed, debated, and ultimately written down—articulated as a program-wide frame of teacher learning (a mission of sorts) and made visible as it is offered as a scaffold for student teachers. The novice teachers can then be scaffolded into appropriating and adjusting it even as they use it simultaneously to adjust their own incoming dispositions. The resulting construct will be a conscious, evolving professional identity. Presuming that a program's learning frame is opened up to continual critique and reciprocal adjustment, it, too, should become a dynamic, useful programmatic tool: an explicit but loosely defined program identity.

What to Do?
A Series of Suggestions for Teacher Education

Embrace integration. Holistic approaches to practice logically result from ecological research. We should acknowledge the epistemological interconnectedness of all parts of the teacher development process. We should accept that knowledge is a wide and active process, and that learning involves multidimensional changes in multilayered ways coming from multiple sources. Enacted in programs, these assumptions will encourage usefully holistic treatments of teacher development.

Foreground a view of knowledge construction as recursive and personalized. This study illustrates some of the ways in which a novice teacher's biography, personal relationships, and cultural positionings affect the way professional knowledge develops. Teacher educators might wish to place this learning perspective close to the center of their approaches. Foregrounding the fact that student teachers are assembling their own teacher professional identities rather than acquiring expert knowledge should increase the authenticity of the teacher education experience.

Encourage knowledge conflicts yet do not withhold sufficient program support and follow-through. Teacher education might find better ways to encourage prospective teachers to deeply interrogate their own assumptions, get into knowledge conflicts, and get out of those conflicts. Though difficult, it remains a deserving goal and one whose benefits warrant the time and energy required.

Seek a coherent vision (without sacrificing heterodoxy). Structurally fragmented teacher education programs offer a body of knowledge that sometimes appears contradictory and/or diffuse. This can render it defenseless against the stronger, more deeply embedded prior identities held by teacher candidates. Instead, a program might wish to seek consensus on what it expects graduates to know and do, and explicitly collaborate on ways to achieve those output standards. Yet, there is still the cardinal need to allow—encourage, even—heterogeneity of ideas and goals for teacher education. Coherence is in some ways necessary and useful but must be treated carefully: It should never stand as tacit proxy for censorship over diverse opinions or thoughtful critique.

Pursue holistic practice and ecological research around teacher identity. We should discard simplistic notions of knowledge as merely intellectual, learning as abstract, knowing as linear, and teacher development as the direct internalization of new ideas. Each of these tenets descends from faulty premises and misunderstands the situated, holistic nature of learning to teach. Embracing the reconceptualization put forth by this book will encourage more sensitive, more meaningful teacher preparation.

Drawing from George Mead (1964/1932), Mikhail Bakhtin (in Holquist 1990), and Dorothy Holland et al. (1998), I locate "teacher identity" inside cultural studies of the person. This angle of inquiry departs from traditional psychological frames of identity, which treat individuals as autonomous, purposeful, and fixed (e.g., Erickson 1980/1959). It also avoids the overemphasis on macrostructural influences (like race, class, and gender), which dominate modernist sociological and anthropological framings. Instead, the sociocultural model of identity I advocate considers that people both are products of their social histories and—through things like hope, desperation, imagining, and mindfulness—move themselves from one subjectivity to the next, from one facet of their identity to another, and can in some limited sense choose to act in certain ways considered by them to be coherent with their own self-understandings. Teacher identity is both a product and a process. As a product, it is the collection of influences and effects on a teacher. And yet it is also a process—a way of viewing the continuous interaction among active variables that constitutes teacher development. I view identity as a label, really, for the collection of influences and effects from immediate contexts, prior constructs of self, social positionings, and meaning systems (each itself a fluid influence and all together an ever-changing construct) that become intertwined inside the flow of activity as a teacher simultaneously reacts to and negotiates given contexts and human relationships at given moments. Foregrounding teacher identity research will encourage us to better capture and understand the complexity of learning and teaching in situ. Methodologies like teacher interview/analysis, ethnography, narrative analysis, and action research—along with critical modes of analysis that foreground identity studies—should continue to deepen the field's understanding of how teachers develop and how who one is as a person interacts with who one is as a teacher. This is how teacher education can continue to matter as it simultaneously improves its ways of supporting quality teaching and teacher retention.

Notes

1. And again, as discussed in chapter one, I do not mean to deny post-structuralist notions of coherence as a false myth, or the concept that opposites juxtaposed are a (not unhealthy) feature of postmodern existence (Lemert 1997). My point here is that, typically, a person strives for his or her apparent version of a coherence that offers harmony enough to maintain relative sanity.

2. Such a perspective supports claims for professional development schools (Darling-Hammond, Wise, and Klein 1995; Lieberman 1995) and views of teacher development as a career-long continuum in which early phases like

recruitment and teacher preparation are inextricable from induction, professional development, and teacher retention (Olsen and Anderson 2007; Sykes 1999).

3. I use these two broader conceptions of personality because they downplay strict demarcations between heredity and environment and therefore encourage ecological treatments of self. Bourdieu's (1991) sociological "habitus" is also a helpful formulation as it links status, sociohistory, and self-formation.

4. I know I am on shaky ground here for several reasons. One is that I am no expert in Eastern thought. A second is that the essence of Zen is that what is most important is ungraspable: that truth is an unknowable essence rather than some two-dimensional set of premises and conclusions; that the more you talk the less you know, the more you know the less you understand; that any attempt to explain truth necessarily sends it running. Zen thrives on paradoxes, and so any explanation of it is self-defeating.

Appendix

Studying Teacher Development
Research Methods and Methodology

Theory is a process, an ever-developing entity, not a perfected product.

—Glaser and Strauss

Research Design

This qualitative research project created and intertwined several empirically developed case studies to analyze the iterative processes of knowledge construction by which eight teacher candidates became beginning teachers. Data were collected over a two-year period, while data analysis required another two years. The approach was decidedly inductive—the shape of my thinking changing as I became more familiar with the unfolding experiences of the study participants. I chose an inductive approach for two related reasons: because keeping my mind open at the beginning would limit the data-collection-as-self-fulfilling-prophecy bias, and because the analytical approach I ultimately adopted was allowed to emerge organically from the empirical data. It seems to me that the best qualitative research—participating in grounded theory, made of iterative explorations back and forth into data and explanation-building—is both inductive and deductive. Inductively, the researcher begins with empirical specifics and moves outward toward larger patterns and themes. Deductively, the researcher first learns the existing research landscape and considers, rejects, confirms, and adjusts it in relation to new data in order to extend the research conversation. That these two complementary procedures join up while the analysis is being conducted offers an elegant symmetry.

During the summer of 1998, I purposefully selected four northern California secondary education teacher credentialing programs that in the aggregate loosely resembled the local sample of Bay Area university teacher preparation options:

- Two large, public, nonselective, inexpensive programs
- One midsized, private, highly selective, expensive program
- One small, public, highly selective, medium expensive program

All four placed their student teachers in predominantly urban and urban fringe settings. Through stratified random selection, I chose two teacher candidates (English concentration) from each program. One candidate from each program was intended to resemble the "typical" teacher candidate (Lanier and Little 1986; Lortie 1975; NCES n.d.; Wideen, Mayer-Smith, and Moon 1998). This typical teacher candidate was—according to demographic research—a white, young twenties, middle-class woman from a suburban or rural location who speaks only English. There were other, less observable characteristics identified in the available research, but I was not able to make use of them. They included having chosen their profession before age eighteen (Lortie 1975; NCES n.d.), tending to like children, skewing Judeo-Christian in their upbringing (if not in beliefs), tending to teach within one hundred miles of their birthplace (Wideen, Mayer-Smith, and Moon 1998), tending to have been moderately successful in school (Wideen, Mayer-Smith, and Moon 1998), tending to be humanistic and generally conformist (Wideen, Mayer-Smith, and Moon 1998), and tending to score in the lowest quartile of the SAT and the National Teachers Exam (Lanier and Little 1986).

The other candidate from each program was intended to resemble the farthest deviation from the "typical" teacher candidate that population constraints would allow. I was interested in including this category of teacher candidate because it would allow for the opportunity to contrast demographic aspects as influences on learning to teach, and carried the potential to generate additional culture-related themes affecting the professional development of beginning teachers. The characteristics I chose to consider were the following (in no particular order):

- Age
- Race and/or ethnicity

- Gender
- Native language
- Birthplace
- Educational background
- Previous employment experience
- Prior experience working with kids

This distance between typical candidate and farthest deviation differed according to the population constraints of each program. I was limited by the fact that most English teacher candidates in all four programs were white young women. In these four programs, there were only three candidates of color; I chose one of them. At each site, then, this "farthest deviation" reflected the greatest distance allowable. At one site this meant a young woman born in Iran who speaks Farsi first and English second (my one candidate of color). At another site this meant a forty-nine-year-old man changing careers. At a third site this meant a thirty-eight-year-old man in a wheelchair. At the fourth site this meant simply a male from outside California.

In order to protect against self-selection bias, I did not seek volunteers but rather introduced my project to each program cohort, addressing each group on their first day of class and requesting that anyone uninterested in participating put their name on a piece of paper and place it inside an envelope I left in each room (only one did). From the remaining pool, I looked at whatever biographical information was available (undergraduate education information, previous work experience, matriculation materials), talked with program directors (to learn more about individual candidates), considered observable characteristics (race, gender, approximate age), and invited my choices to participate. All agreed, though one candidate exited during the second year. I was not affiliated with any of the teacher education programs and did not previously know any of the candidates I selected; I consciously chose to place myself as close to the observer pole of the observer/participant continuum because I wanted the data collected to be as objective a portrait of the eight candidates as was possible.[1]

Data Collection (1998–2000)

Data collection during the first year consisted of eight open-ended, tape-recorded, sixty- to ninety-minute conversations with each of the candidates; shadowing candidates in their teacher education classes and meetings and writing "thick description" (Ryle, quoted in Geertz 1973) field notes; observing candidates in their student teacher classrooms (again, producing field notes); and collecting official and unofficial documents and artifacts from programs and candidates. I also rigorously kept a research journal. I was interested in knowing the candidates as people, as teachers, as students of teaching; capturing their conceptions of teaching, learning, and schooling; and collecting interpretations of their teacher education program, their learning-to-teach experiences, and their (continually changing) identities. I was also interested in monitoring my own reflexive roles and emerging understandings of the topic. Some interviews were completely open-ended: a conversation initiated with the question "So, what's new?" and interrupted only to probe for further information, clarification, or concrete examples. Other interviews followed loosely constructed protocols, asking interviewees to tell life stories, conduct think-alouds, define and describe concepts, talk through card sorts, or respond to specific questions. To capture conceptions and approaches of the program and program staff, I collected data from the programs themselves: faculty and administrator interviews, class meeting observations, official and unofficial documents and artifacts. Because I sought natural data, I rarely asked respondents directly to discuss their knowledge sources: I wanted answers to emerge indirectly in context and in conjunction with observations of practice. This aided me in avoiding scripted responses or speakers offering the responses they thought I wanted to hear.

During the second semester of their first year, I concentrated primarily on the student teaching experience, because that was each program's focus. Observing and writing about the candidates in their classrooms; collecting their various teaching artifacts, journals, and lesson plans; and allowing them to direct the tape-recorded conversations all allowed me to capture student teaching and learning-to-teach *emically,* as they were experiencing it. At the end of the school year, I conducted a last round of interviews, this time asking informants to recount biographies and life stories.

During the second year, I continued to observe the candidates teaching, conducted tape-recorded conversations with them, and collected official and unofficial documents. In the late spring, I shadowed each candidate through two consecutive workdays and then conducted a final debriefing interview at the end of our second full day together.

All interviews were transcribed. I maintained my research journal. My database is represented in Table A.1.

Analysis (1999–2002)

Because I adopted a multidisciplinary research approach, my analytical methods vary. Embedded in my approach to studying the data are perspectives and procedures from three analytical paradigms: *epistemology* (which itself sits inside traditions of psychology, anthropology, and philosophy), *critical theory* (a sometimes Marxian and sometimes postmodern blend of sociology, anthropology, literary analysis, and philosophy), and *sociolinguistics* (introduced in what follows). The analytical process was continuous, consisting of several overlapping, sequenced phases, each of which used various perspectives, theories, and procedures from the traditions presented above to understand the data. By "understand the data," I mean the ability to (1) extract

Table A.1 Study Database

Interview transcripts from conversations	"Thick description" field notes from observations	Official documents	Other artifacts
• with eight candidates	• of program classes	• program materials (handbooks, descriptions, handouts)	• notes and e-mails from candidates
• with six program coordinators	• of program meetings		• card sorts
• with five program instructors and supervisors	• of candidate teaching classes	• course materials (syllabi, handouts, guides)	• pre-study and post-study surveys
	• of school site meetings	• candidates' coursework	• Internet data on participating schools and university programs
		• candidates' unit and lesson plans, teaching artifacts	

from the data thematic patterns that were in some bounded way generalizable to the sample; (2) depict each of these teachers as holistic learners in case studies and cross-case portraits; and (3) build a richly theorized, empirically built account of beginning teacher knowledge development.

Because my intent was to understand how beginning teachers construct their professional knowledge, I was interested primarily in *process.* I put my faith in the process narrative because it highlights the occurrence of events in actual contexts under conditions that, in the aggregate, compose the logic—or story—in which the phenomena exist (Becker 1998; Gardner 1993). This means that I do not seek direct causality: As Becker writes, "[P]rocess narratives don't have predestined goals" (Becker 1998, 62).

Analytical Phases

Phase one of data analysis was a preliminary content analysis of the collected data—reviewing approximately two thousand pages of interview transcripts, one hundred pages of field notes, and three boxes of documents and artifacts. This review process allowed me to recognize and catalog topics, and begin systematizing those key words, patterns, and personal understandings that were emerging, and that would later become helpful analytical entryways into the data (Becker 1998; Linde 1993; Miles and Huberman 1984; Woods 1996). It was during this analytical phase that I created a preliminary theoretical model of teacher knowledge construction. This model changed and deepened during subsequent phases of analysis; it ultimately became the theoretical model of teacher learning I present near the end of chapter one.

Phase two focused on drawing from that content analysis to generate preliminary coding categories and data sampling strategies in preparation for finer-grained analysis. Those initial categories and subcategories are shown in Table A.2.

My goal for data sampling was twofold: I wanted to reduce the amount of raw data to analyze, and I wanted to generate a useful, yet representative, subset with which I could investigate my research questions. Ultimately, I selected four teachers whose experiences I write about in this book: one teacher from each of the four programs. These cases were selected because, in the aggregate, they reflect the broadest range of possible experience with programs. Kim wholly rejected her program;

Table A.2 Preliminary Coding Categories

I. Influences coming from the self
    a. Self-perceptions from candidates
    b. My perceptions of their personality traits
    c. Informant conceptions of the personal nature of teaching

II. Influences coming from cultural positionings
    a. Gender
    b. Sexual orientation
    c. Socioeconomic status
    d. Ethnicity and race
    e. Epistemes (Foucault 1970, 1972)
    f. Home/family

III. Influences coming from previous experiences
    a. In home/family
    b. As kindergarten through grade eight student
    c. As high school student
    d. As college student
    e. Observing teachers
    f. Working with young people
    g. Miscellaneous

IV. Influences coming from teacher education program
    a. Program faculty/coursework
    b. Mentor teachers
    c. Program culture/ethos
    d. Student teaching experience
    e. Seminar meetings
    f. Peers/collegiality

V. Informants' conceptions
    a. of subject of English
    b. of teaching
    c. of program
    d. of teaching practicum
    e. of students
    f. of learning and knowledge
    g. of schooling and society
    h. of first-year teaching
    i. of own self/identity (and changes)
    j. of colleagues and collegial nature of learning/schooling
    k. of reasons for entry into profession

---

[1] I use "self" and "personality" interchangeably, linking them using Hamachek's (1999) notion of personality as the collection of given-off personal characteristics presented to others as a "self." Another useful term is Gardner's (1993) "personality configuration."

William fully embraced his; and Azar and Liz both appropriated program knowledges to fit their own goals and conceptions, but they did so in different ways. I make no claims for typicality; certainly different pre-service teachers will have different professional development experiences (that is the point of this study!). Instead, my research design was about investigating ways in which different candidate characteristics interrelated with different programmatic characteristics, and what those ultimate learning processes looked like in practice.

I chose to include transcripts from all program faculty interviews as supplementary data, not as material for fine-grained analysis, because the programs and instructors themselves were not the primary focus of this study. Likewise, I chose to closely analyze all documents from the teacher candidates but to treat documents and artifacts from the programs as supplementary. Finally, I included all field notes from all my observations and drew from the research journal in which I had been regularly writing.

Phase three was a fine-grained analysis of the remaining data. Following advice from Peter Woods (1996) and Barney Glaser and Anselm Strauss (1967, cited in Woods 1996), I considered "theory" as a process, not a perfected product, and approached this phase as essentially a never-ending work in progress (cut off, finally, by the pragmatic need to finish the dissertation and graduate). This phase included two years of recursive analyses of field notes, interview transcripts, and collected documents in order to generate the findings reported in this book. To conduct these two years of data study, I relied primarily on sociolinguistics as analytic method.

Using Sociolinguistic Methods to Uncover Speaker Meaning in Teacher Interview Transcripts[2]

To understand the collected interview data, I relied on an extended analysis of language use and the conceptions, representations, and perspectives language use reveals. Specifically, I employed text analysis, conversation analysis, and discourse analysis methods to build portraits of the teachers as learners. The decision to rely primarily on sociolinguistic forms of analysis resulted from my conviction that it is primarily through language that individuals enact and present themselves and their (often socially constructed) knowledge to each other (Cazden 1988; Fairclough 1989; Gee 1999; Goffman 1959; Gumperz 1982). As Hans-Georg Gadamer writes, "Being, that can be understood, is language" (in Grondin 1994, xiv). Humans rely on language—spoken, written, enacted, or even, in the case of semiotics, symbolized—to interpret the world, navigate the world, reveal and construct themselves inside the world, and position themselves (or get positioned) in the world. Language both shapes people and is shaped by them. Language exists *inside* the social world: In other words, diction, meanings, and ways in which language is used are not independent, autonomous processes but social activities imbued with the multiple social influences that mark all human contexts and histories (Bourdieu 1991; Fairclough 1989; Foucault 1970; Freire 1987; Gee 1992; Luke 1995). Thus, language is social practice. It bridges the cognitive with the social, the individual with the cultural (Barnes, in Cazden 1988). As Courtney Cazden (1988) explains, language exists to communicate information (propositional function), establish and maintain social relationships (social function), and express a speaker's identity and attitudes (expressive function). Additionally, Norman Fairclough's (1989) notion of "subject positions" holds that over time individuals, through language use, embody the various ways the world positions them even as they, in part, inscribe those same positionings. From early thinkers of linguistics and sociology like Ferdinand de Saussure and Roland Barthes to literary deconstructionists like Umberto Eco and Jacques Derrida comes emphasis on "the linguistic turn" in postmodern history—the point when the social foundation of words and meanings was formally recognized (Derrida 1971; Lemert 1997; Lyotard 1984/1979; Natoli and Hutcheon 1993).

The words of the teachers I interviewed interested me not as ends in themselves, but as the means through which they revealed their knowledge, their meaning-perspectives, and their interpretations of their own developing teacher identities. I presumed that there exist several dimensions of relationship among their knowledge, the ways they talk about their practice, and how they enact teaching and learning in context. I further presumed that an investigator can isolate and uncover many of those features of any teacher's meaning system by studying how teachers talk about themselves, talk about teaching, and talk about their experiences.[3]

There are multiple methodological traditions of examining language in use—the loose cluster known as sociolinguistics—and they derive from diverse disciplines, including anthropology, rhetoric, literary criticism, philosophy, psychology, and sociology. The treatment I adopted for my study comes primarily from discourse analysis—itself a cluster of related sociolinguistic analyses that share the common presumption that speakers and hearers typically cooperate in unspoken ways in order to maintain conversation. This means there is an order, or an internal logic, to conversants' language use that can be identified and examined. Other treatments (for example, intercultural communication theory [e.g., Gudykunst et al. 1996; Scollon and Scollon 2001] and interactional models of communication [e.g., Gumperz 1982]) focus on the *unshared* cultural-linguistic assumptions often characterizing cross-cultural miscommunication, because these treatments focus on groups from different speech communities attempting to converse together. Because each of my informants was participating, more or less, in the same cultural community as I was, I decided I could employ discourse analysis. Though I will return to this point later, it should be remembered that most discourse analysis methods require that investigators first consider and establish ways speakers are or are not operating from the same assumptions about culture and language. To presume conversants across speech communities rely on similar assumptions is to misunderstand the situated nature of sociolinguistics.

My discourse analysis procedures were varied as, I believe, first, that different kinds of text require different methods of analysis, and second, that the choice of analytical method depends on what questions one intends to ask of the data.[4] This first point is a structural one. It means that, for example, a long monologue might be examined through the lens of a code systems approach that allows us to presume that, accounting for context and purpose, a speaker's words more or less directly reflect his or her thoughts on the subject (Schiffrin 1994). The second point is functional, and means that different research purposes necessitate different analytical methods. For example, because I was interested in examining sources of professional knowledge for the teachers I studied, I asked informants to describe their pasts and tell stories from their present. The contents of these stories I could examine through the lens of a life story approach to creating coherence through narrative. Charlotte Linde (1993) reports on the various coherence systems her interviewees employed (those of psychology, behaviorism, feminism, the Catholic confessional) as they offered explanations, told stories, and chronicled personal events. I, too, extracted embedded coherence systems teachers relied on to explain and tell their stories and, in so doing, was provided a glimpse into the interpretive (and simultaneously epistemological and ontological) frames through which these beginning teachers were constructing and revealing their professional knowledge, their conceptions of self, and their interpretations of context.

Positionality and Interpretive Research

If adult learning is indeed a process of assembling knowledge using interpretive constructs deriving from prior experience inside social positionings, then I, too, must be at least partly under the spell of my past. This means that my study was a conscious exercise in self-analysis, as well. I was obliged to identify and consider embedded ways in which I conceived of learning, teaching, knowledge, and interpretive research. I needed to examine ways in which my own power as a researcher or positioning vis-à-vis interviewees shaped the teachers' talk. I tried to be reflexive and careful to delimit the amount of my bias that seeped into the analysis. I had colleagues discuss my coding categories and approaches with me. Whenever possible, I had them critically deconstruct my emerging procedures, findings, and paths of inference. I employed member checks, going over parts of prior transcripts with interviewees to discuss their responses and my interpretations with them. During my analysis of interviews, I critiqued my findings to test for alternative explanations.

I had no prior contact with any of the informants of this study. I was not involved in any of their preparation programs. I was an outside researcher who negotiated access to four university teacher education programs and used stratified random sampling to select informants. Of course, the teachers and I developed personal relationships that included power dynamics, various assumptions, and multiple subject positions. These needed to be consciously considered. I was an education researcher who had also been a high school English teacher. This meant that I was reasonably facile with the jargon of the academy within education and that I had practical experience in the very domain for which these teachers were preparing themselves. I also made sure to recognize and attend to influences from gender, personality, and culture.

To expose and make all of these variables part of the study, I discussed these issues with interviewees and compared these conversations with others we had. During interviews, I frequently asked the teachers what they actually meant by terms they used (like *constructivism* or *knowing*), trying to encourage them to unpack the lexicon of teaching into personalized explanations of meaning. And I always probed for concrete examples or connections to what I had observed so I could better learn how and where they located their explanations. I approached topics from multiple angles, using different phrasings over the two years. My intent with these procedures was to never assume I knew precisely how they were using terms; this stance created additional opportunities for them to reveal knowledge as they discussed what they meant by terms such as *theory, curriculum,* or *political,* or told a story about two students and a newspaper article to illustrate what was meant by "doing a fishbowl." Finally, I employed a separate analysis of the interviews solely to examine ways that my role as researcher affected the conversations and subsequent analyses. Despite these efforts, some bias no doubt seeped in: This is one limitation of the research approach. As with most interpretive work, the findings are open, in part, to interpretation. I discuss other limitations at the end of this appendix.

Two Models of Viewing Communication

To study the interview transcripts, I relied primarily on analyses existing within two basic treatments of communication—what Deborah Schiffrin (1994) calls the *code model* and the *inferential model.* (There is a third model, the *interactional model,* which I did not employ but which I will discuss later.) The code model presumes that a speaker possesses an "internally represented proposition (a thought) that he or she intends to make accessible to another person" and, by transforming the thought into mutually understood signals (the sounds or marks we know as words), communicates the thought to someone who—relying upon the same understanding of those mutually understood signals—retrieves and decodes the message and therefore receives the intended thought (Schiffrin 1994, 391). This more or less direct interpretation of communication, simply put, takes a person's words as prima facie representations of his or her intended propositions. Used carefully, this model has value. I used this approach to look at relatively unproblematic monologues spoken by informants within a tape-recorded conversation.[5] The following sample from my first interview with Liz is one example:

> BRAD: Assuming you could have gone into a classroom as a teacher through an emergency certification or as a substitute, why did you choose to go through a [university credentialing] program?

Liz: I don't want to hate something. I'm excited about it. I want to do it, and I want to do it well, and I don't want to be so frightened and intimidated by it that I don't like it. I know that one year is not going to prepare you for what it's really like when you walk into a classroom, but I want the illusion of confidence of a foundation, and that that will be enough to make me feel like I know that I'm doing enough. It's probably just a facade or something that I would convince myself of. I think that in most respects performance is based on confidence. If you're a singer in a band, it doesn't matter if you're good or not. It's what you bring to that, and I think that's true of teaching. If you inspire that trust and respect because it's something you think that you're good at, then that will be enough to stand on.

Although a bit of inferential analysis is required (How did the phrasing of my question perhaps shape her answer? What assumptions does she take as shared between us? What aspects of our relationship might she be appealing to?), much of her response can be interpreted as her beliefs and thoughts directly communicated. This means that I can use the passage to posit the following preliminary propositions Liz believes true:

1. That without the teacher education experience, she would be so frightened and intimidated by teaching that she would hate it;[6]
2. That one year of preparation is insufficient for the demands of actual teaching, but that it is sufficient for providing the *illusion* of confidence, and that is enough to get started;
3. That, in most respects, performance is based on confidence, and in this regard teaching is like singing in a band;
4. That confidence inspires trust and respect from others and allows others to believe (legitimately or not) that one is a good teacher or singer.

I used these tentative conclusions and others like them to begin creating my understanding of Liz as a teacher. Alone, they do not carry the full evidentiary warrant. The code model is an approach best used in conjunction with the inferential model, described below, and a rigorous reflexiveness. However, these preliminary assertions contribute to the findings. Using various coding categories (in this case, reasons for entry, initial expectations for her teacher preparation experience, thoughts about the relationship between confidence and teaching, teaching as performance), I cataloged the information about Liz for later analysis. My developing portrait was being adjusted, confirmed, reconstructed—and over time assembled into a set of conclusive findings about Liz and her experience.

The second model of communication I relied on as I analyzed discourse is the inferential model. This model more strongly highlights shared subjectivity within communication; in other words, it places in the foreground the fact that speaker and hearer rely on shared understandings as they maintain meaningful conversation. The code model, of course, also relies on shared subjectivity—accurately encoding and decoding language requires implicit agreement of code meanings—yet, the inferential model places its focus squarely on the notion of shared intentions structuring meaningful conversation. It focuses on *intentionality* as the basis of language use, presuming we communicate our intentions (not only our attitudes and beliefs) through our words and our interpretations of the words of others.

However, just because the inferential model presupposes shared subjectivity does not mean it always expects it. Several discourse analytic techniques are as interested in when and why conversations break down as they are in why they are sustained. Discourse analysts posit that maintaining conversational involvement "requires that certain linguistic and sociocultural knowledge needs to be shared" (Schiffrin 1994, 103). When communication is successful, it is because knowledge is shared and (often implicitly) understood by participants. When communication fails, it is due to a breach in the unspoken assumptions. Accepting this set of premises allows investigators to look at the language use—the linguistic patterns—in order to uncover and examine both the shared assumptions and the unshared ones, and the meaning systems underneath. Yet, this also means that a language researcher must identify the various interpretive frames within which speakers are located and make analytical decisions accordingly. One's choice of analytical approach should be aligned with the features of the research context, the speech communities of the participants, and the particular questions one wishes to ask of the data.

The notion of communication across speech communities raises a third treatment of language, called the interactional model of communication. This treatment deemphasizes intersubjectivity, instead highlighting ways in which a hearer's interpretation of language might not align with the speaker's intentions. This is a treatment that reveals ways in which speakers, to use Erving Goffman's words, "give off" as much (or more) information as they "give" during conversations (Goffman 1959). It is a model that examines the often *unintended communication* speakers reveal as they engage in social situations: Examples include body language, what is not said, the direction of one's gaze, pitch changes, and so on. John Gumperz's (1982) work on speech communities investigated places in which conversation broke down when intercultural assumptions were unshared. Stanley Fish (1986) coined the term *interpretive communities* to illuminate how speakers, readers, and hearers rely on interpretive boundaries linked to cultural-linguistic assumptions that account for understandings and misunderstandings when using language. Interactional sociolinguistics—as some of these analyses are labeled—presumes communication is not always shared and places its analytical emphasis on context and culture (e.g., Goffman 1959, 1981; Gumperz 1982). I want to return, however, to the inferential model in order to use a discussion of one of its examples—pragmatics—to illustrate my primary approach to analyzing interview transcripts.

Using Pragmatics to Infer Meaning from Interview Transcripts

Philosopher H. P. Grice (1968, 1975) developed ideas about how conversants cooperate in patterned ways in order to sustain conversation. His ideas shaped an approach to discourse called *pragmatics*. The nonnatural meaning component of Gricean pragmatics allows that we can assume intentionality on the part of the speaker—that a comment is "intended to be recognized in a particular way by a recipient" (Schiffrin 1994, 193). However, Gricean pragmatics postulates a second intention, too: that the recipient also recognizes the speaker's intention (Grice 1975). Speaker and hearer cooperate in unspoken ways in order to maintain coherence within conversation. Grice named this cooperative principle "implicature." Grice's notion of implicature allows that a speaker's meaning comes partly out of examining how the subsequent hearer reacted to the comment. This continues as the hearer then becomes next speaker and the initial speaker becomes a hearer reacting to the comment. These back-and-forth occurrences of mutually understood intentions sustain meaningful conversation and, as a consequence, allow a researcher to presume comments can be accepted as reflections of conversants' intentions. For example, imagine I am a stranger who approaches you on a street with a gas can in hand and asks, "Do you know where the nearest gas station is?" You reply, "I'm not from here. But I've got a siphon, and my car is nearby." From this short exchange, a researcher can infer that you understood my question (even though you did not literally "answer" it) and that you do not know where any nearby gas station is (because if you did, you would have answered differently), and you feel the need (politeness? to compensate for not knowing?) to offer an explanation for why you do not know where the nearest gas station is (if you were responding rudely with a sarcastic cue, you would probably not have followed with an offer of help). Further, the researcher can presume that you have understood why I desire a gas station and that you believe it accurate and acceptable to offer your car and siphon (which is no gas station at all). Understanding the intentions embedded in what you have said, I then answer, "Great. Thanks." This is implicature. It allows us to understand how conversation is not always—or not merely—about the exchange of literal meanings of words.

Let me present an example from the data. During an interview I told Liz that, because I was once an English teacher, I have files of lesson plan ideas I would be willing to loan her sometime. Her reply was a sudden "Do you have grammar stuff?" which got us talking about the teaching of grammar. At one point, the following exchange occurred:

> BRAD: And, with students, there's so much baggage that comes with the word *grammar* that when that *Warriner's* comes out, immediately people are ready to hate whatever you're going to do.

> LIZ: I think the biggest problem is that it's never taught in context. You never see why it's of value to know how this thing [a sentence] is built. Somehow, I think I could make it interesting.

In this short exchange, I make a claim that students rarely enjoy being taught grammar, especially by way of the traditional *Warriner's* grammar series. Hearing my comment, and interpreting the pause at its end as an entreaty for her to speak, Liz was suddenly faced with a broad range of possible responses. She could talk about students or teachers or herself; she could break "grammar" up into constituent parts by talking about one example or piece of grammar; she could address my reference to *Warriner's*; she could disregard the importance of grammar altogether; she could go off on an unrelated tangent; she could take exception to all or part of what I have said. This list of possible replies is nearly inexhaustible. When, however, she chooses one response, Liz reveals valuable clues about herself. She reveals how she interprets my comments and she reveals embedded conceptions and intentions of her own about aspects of teaching, learning, and grammar instruction.

By examining the cultural and contextual cues present, the referents used, the way her words relate to mine, and the lexical and syntactic choices she makes, I can hypothesize various attitudes, conceptions, orientations, and beliefs that Liz appears to hold about teaching grammar. When tested against other passages within and across the interviews, my field notes, and collected teaching artifacts, these hypotheses become stronger or weaker, confirmed or discounted, adjusted and refined. As more and more of the interviews are analyzed, this collection of hypotheses becomes larger in quantity and stronger in assertion and, ultimately, becomes the findings I further analyzed and finally reported. As example, we can look closely at Liz's language use in this passage just presented. Here it is again:

> BRAD: And, with students, there's so much baggage that comes with the word *grammar* that when that *Warriner's* comes out, immediately people are ready to hate whatever you're going to do.
>
> LIZ: I think the biggest problem is that it's never taught in context. You never see why it's of value to know how this thing [a sentence] is built. Somehow, I think I could make it interesting.

In response to my assertion, Liz chooses to announce that she believes the primary "problem" (the reason why students do not like the study of grammar) is that "it's never taught in context." Because she has not asked me about *Warriner's* (I know from other interviews that she typically interrupts me to ask for clarification when she does not understand a word or concept I use; further, she has referenced *Warriner's* before) we can presume she knows what *Warriner's* is. Because her comment built off of mine, rather than contradicting or disagreeing with mine, we can presume she accepts that students often "hate" being taught grammar. From her particular phrasing ("the biggest problem is"), we can infer that Liz believes there's an identifiable primary reason—out of several "less big" ones—why students hate the study of grammar and that the reason corresponds to the notion of teaching grammar out of context. And she reveals something about her conception of context and teaching grammar immediately after, when she directly follows her comment about context by saying, "You never see why it's of value to know how this thing is built. Somehow, I think I could make it interesting." By analyzing her use of "you," the uses of "it," the verb "see," the noun phrase "this thing," and by applying the notion of implicature to her comments, we can deduce several general assertions Liz intends to make. Her comment in these lines reveals that she believes *teaching grammar in context* entails (1) communicating to students how sentences are formed in order to (2) demonstrate the value of knowing how sentences are formed. And it reveals, (3) that to do so would make the study of grammar "interesting" to students (and therefore not hated by them) and, finally, (4) that she believes she can do such a thing, but—look at her use of "somehow"—she is not yet sure how to do it. Such an analysis, then, allows me to tentatively posit several specific, related premises Liz must presume as true in order to say what she said and expect it to be understood by me (more or less) as she intended it. The premises are these:

1. That there is more than one reason why students hate learning grammar, but the articulated one is the primary one;
2. If it is demonstrated to a student how a sentence is built, the student will see the value of learning grammar;
3. If the student understands the value of grammar (as conceived of in previous premise), he or she will no longer hate the study of grammar;
4. That demonstration (e.g., showing how a sentence is built) is a kind of teaching because it leads to appreciation, which, Liz believes, is linked to understanding;
5. That understanding (or learning) is related to noticing or "seeing"; in other words, that noticing a thing leads to understanding or appreciating the thing;
6. That Liz believes she will be able to demonstrate the value of learning grammar by demonstrating how sentences are built and, in so doing, make the study of grammar interesting;
7. That, though she is confident about achieving this kind of teaching just articulated in premise 6, she does not yet know how she will achieve it.

Also interesting is that each of us uses the second-person pronoun "you" to position the hearer in a particular, but different, way. When I say, "whatever you're going to do," I frame her as a hypothetical teacher teaching grammar. She automatically picks this up and also uses the second-person "you," which could suggest that the hearer—me—is a student learning grammar but, because I know she knows I am not such a student, it must more accurately reveal that she believes I am familiar enough with secondary school students to be able to put myself in the place of a student—to pretend for the moment that I am such a student. As my words made us pretend she is a teacher (which, at this point in her preparation program, she was not), her words pretended I was a student. This complementary pair of mutually understood, implied statements underscores the implicature that occurs as we speak. It also acts as analytic lever, because it offers one place where each of us is required to make assumptions about what a student is, and, in fact, Liz's conceptual picture of a student might not resemble my picture at all. This makes it a good location for scrutiny and comparison to other places where Liz talks of students and/or grammar.

Iterative Passes Through the Transcripts Produced Analytical Portraits

Using these methods to illuminate speaker meaning and speakers' reliance on embedded meaning systems allowed me to build portraits of each teacher's process of knowledge construction. It proved time-consuming but productive: Over two years' time (after two years of data collection), I built understandings of each teacher as a three-dimensional learner who relied on prior understandings (coming from life histories, social contexts, and cultural constructions) to interpret and organize teacher preparation experiences into professional knowledge. This is how I came to view the teachers as negotiating their own learning-to-teach processes, which were at once holistic, continuous, and situated. The analytical method I have described here allowed me to examine the speakers' own perspectives and meanings, rather than impose my own. The method pushed me to explore microscopic details of their (and my own) language use to consider how language revealed each of our constructed views of self, world, teaching, and the process of becoming a teacher. And, finally, the method kept me honest by requiring that I continually shift back and forth between the words used in interviews and the meaning I was attaching to those words. This methodological dialectic—made possible by sociolinguistics—was invaluable in uncovering speaker meaning from interview transcripts.

Limitations of This Methodology

Reasons inside primarily three categories shaped the accuracy of this analytical approach. One category is my own bias; I discussed that earlier. The second category is that, because I relied heavily on interview data, there were issues around self-reported data and scripted responses. I had to contend with the worry that interviewees told me what they thought I wanted to hear or presented idealized versions of themselves. Goffman's (1959) "impression management" is relevant here: Individuals sometimes manage the impressions others have of them so as to present themselves in an idealized form. I attempted to protect against this hazard in several ways. Because the data were collected over two years' time, because I approached the same topics from multiple (often indirect) angles, and because I looked for consistency during analysis, I was able on some level to isolate self-serving or scripted responses without neglecting their disconfirmatory potential. But surely I was unable to fully discard or neutralize all of it; this should be kept in mind.

I chose not to reveal my exact hypotheses or specific ways in which I was considering the learning-to-teach process when I spoke with teacher candidates. This is because my work was meant to be inductive (I did not have any formalized hypotheses) and because I did not want to tacitly encourage interviewees to "help me out" by predicting what I wanted to know and providing it. Instead, I told them I was doing inductive, qualitative work to "explore how some pre-service teachers think about, talk about, and do teaching," and described my research questions in general terms, telling them I wanted to "explore how teachers learned to teach."[7] I thought this would be fair both to them (to give them a sense of my study) and to the collection process (lessening their pressure to supply particular kinds of response). Interestingly, none of the candidates seemed to care much about what I was studying; they were more interested in ensuring I understood their responses in the ways they intended. I realize that this methodological stance—carrying with it a degree of secrecy—might strike some as disingenuous, but I believe there is value in maintaining this kind of informant open-endedness in which to elucidate people's perspectives and meaning systems. There are always parts of each of us we cannot see. As Michael Holquist wrote about Mikhail Bakhtin's dialogism: "The very immediacy which defines my being as a self is the same condition that insures I cannot *perceive* my self" (original italics; Holquist 1990, 26).

Finally, the third category is less a methodological limitation than a clarification: Studies like these capture one static snapshot of teachers learning and practicing in a scene that is in fact forever in progress. These teachers were at one particular point in the development of their knowledge. Like Heraclitus's line about never stepping in the same river twice, teacher knowledge construction is a dynamic, continuous process and, already, the conceptions of the eight teachers I studied have surely changed. Because knowledge is not static, there is important potential for teachers to change and grow in the ways they think about and do teaching. As William Faulkner has observed, the past might never in fact be past, but it is also true that no teacher's future is predestined. Sociolinguistics as an analytical tool helped me to uncover and explore this. And it reminded me again and again that the situated meanings teachers construct are complex, multifaceted, and forever in motion.

Notes

1. I realize, of course, that there is no such thing as pure—or "natural"—collected data (see Erickson 1986; Geertz 1973; Hymes 1972). It is my belief that in every nook and cranny of information retrieval and analysis lie multiple places where one's own subjective position colors the data in question. (In fact, in many ways this is the fundamental premise of the study!) But I do believe there are conscious ways one can greatly limit the infusion of researcher bias into the data being collected and analyzed: Separating data collector from data being collected is, for me, one of them. Reflexive analysis is another. Member checks and critical friends are a third. I also realize that there are trade-offs inherent in placing myself close to the observer side rather than the participant side: Intimacy with informants (and therefore a different proximity to data) can be sacrificed in pursuit of less biased data collection.

2. The remainder of this appendix was first published in 2006, as "Using Sociolinguistic Methods to Uncover Speaker Meaning in Teacher Interview Transcripts," *The International Journal of Qualitative Studies in Education* 19(2): 147–161. Permission to reprint this was generously provided.

3. However, I want to be clear that, because I believe teacher knowledge is mostly enacted in actual practice (not in teachers talking about teaching), I triangulated interview findings with two years of observations and collected documents. Because this discussion focuses solely on analyzing interview transcripts, I have left out any discussion of this part of my methods. But, methodologically, I advocate that teacher knowledge is best studied using some

combination of procedures: interviews, observations of practice, analysis of teaching artifacts. For fuller discussions, see Florio-Ruane (2002), Lampert and Ball (1998), and Woods (1996).

4. There are many ways to define *text*; I borrow from Fairclough (1989, 4) the definition he, in turn, borrows from Halliday to define text as simply "a piece of discourse, spoken or written."

5. And I realize that identifying what constitutes "unproblematic" is itself problematic. I considered passages that ran at least ten lines without interruption and that consisted of either direct responses to my prompts or unprompted monologues as unproblematic. I also consciously considered (by memoing and discussing with interviewees and my colleagues) what kinds of cultural and linguistic assumptions were being shared or were opposing each other. Only those passages in which I could confidently presume mostly shared assumptions were employed were categorized as unproblematic.

6. It is interesting that Liz makes the implicit link between competence and satisfaction; these words of hers suggest that, at this point in her development, she is less interested in *being good* at teaching and more interested in *enjoying* it—students as primary beneficiaries of the teacher's competence is absent. This proved a theme of hers (received from her father) and links to Fuller and Bown's (1975) four stages of teaching concern.

7. I offered to share my views of these beginning professionals as teachers and learners, give them copies of whatever I wrote, and tell them everything about the research, but asked that this occur after data collection had been completed. Subsequently, one of the eight teachers asked for the written research findings; one of the teachers asked me to sit down and share my impressions of her teaching practices; and none asked me to tell them more about the project or my research methods.

References

Acker, S., ed. 1991. *Teachers: Gender and Career Failure*. London: Blackwell.

Ammon, Paul. Personal conversation, December 2000.

Anderson, J., L. Reder, J. Greeno, and H. Simon. 2000. "Perspectives on Learning, Thinking and Activity." *Educational Researcher* 29(4): 11–13.

Anderson, L., and T. Bird. 1995. "How Three Prospective Teachers Construed Three Cases of Teaching." *Teaching and Teacher Education* 11(5): 479–499.

Apple, M. 1999. *Power, Meaning, and Identity: Essays in Critical Education Studies*. New York: Peter Lang.

Au, K. H., and K. M. Blake. 2003. "Cultural Identity and Learning to Teach in a Diverse Community: Findings from a Collective Case Study." *Journal of Teacher Education* 54(3): 192.

Avery, P., and C. Walker. 1993. "Prospective Teachers' Perceptions of Ethnic and Gender Differences in Academic Achievement." *Journal of Teacher Education* 44(1): 27–37.

Ballou, D., and M. Podursky. 2000. "Reforming Teacher Preparation and Licensing: What Is the Evidence?" *Teachers College Record* 102(1): 5–27.

Banks, J. 2002. *An Introduction to Multicultural Education*. Boston: Allyn and Bacon.

Barry, N., and J. Lechner. 1995. "Pre-Service Teachers' Attitudes About and Awareness of Multicultural Teaching and Learning." *Teaching and Teacher Education* 11(20): 149–161.

Becker, H. 1998. *Tricks of the Trade*. Chicago: University of Chicago Press.

Belenky, M., B. Clinchy, N. Goldberger, and J. Tarule. 1986. *Women's Ways of Knowing: The Development of Self, Voice, and Mind*. New York: Basic Books.

Bird, T., L. Anderson, B. Sullivan, and S. Swidler, 1993. "Pedagogical Balancing Acts: Attempts to Influence Prospective Teachers' Beliefs." *Teacher and Teacher Education* 9(3): 253–267.

Blattner, B., K. Hall, and R. Reinhard. 1997. *Facilities and Class Size Reduction*. Sacramento: School Services of California.

Bogdan, R. C., and S. K. Biklen. 1998. *Qualitative Research for Education: An Introduction to Theory and Methods.* Boston: Allyn and Bacon.

Borich, G. 1999. "Dimensions of Self That Influence Effective Teaching." In *The Role of Self in Teacher Development,* edited by R. Lipka and T. Brinthaupt, 92–117. Albany: State University of New York Press.

Bourdieu, P. 1991. *Language and Symbolic Power.* Cambridge, MA: Harvard University Press.

Britzman, D. 1986. "Cultural Myths and the Teacher: Biography and Social Structure in Teacher Education." *Harvard Educational Review* 56(4): 442–456.

———. 1991. *Practice Makes Practice: A Critical Study of Learning to Teach.* Albany: State University of New York Press.

Bruner, J. 1974. *Toward a Theory of Instruction.* Cambridge, MA: Harvard University Press.

———. 1990. *Acts of Meaning.* Cambridge, MA: Harvard University Press.

Bryk, A., V. Lee, and P. Holland. 1993. *Catholic Schools and the Common Good.* Cambridge, MA: Harvard University Press.

Buber, M. 1974. *I and Thou.* New York: Macmillan Publishing Company.

Calderhead, J. 1988. "The Development of Knowledge Structures in Learning to Teach." In *'Teachers' Professional Learning,* edited by James Calderhead, 51–64. Philadelphia, PA: Falmer Press.

California Commission on Teacher Credentialing. 1997. "California Standards for Teaching." Sacramento: California Department of Education.

Campbell, J. 1988. *The Power of Myth* (with Bill Moyers). New York: Anchor Books Doubleday.

———. 1991. *Reflections on the Art of Living: A Joseph Campbell Companion.* New York: HarperPerennial.

Carroll, S. J., R. E. Reichardt, C. M. Guarino, and A. Mejia. 2000. "The Distribution of Teachers Among California's School Districts and Schools." Paper No. MR-1298.0-JIF. Santa Monica, CA: RAND.

Cazden, C. 1988. *Classroom Discourse.* Portsmouth, NH: Heinemann.

Clandinin, D. J. 1985. "Personal Practical Knowledge: A Study of Teachers' Classroom Images." *Curriculum Inquiry* 15(4): 361–385.

Clandinin, D. J., and M. Connelly. 1995. *Teachers' Professional Knowledge Landscapes.* New York: Teachers College Press.

Clark, C. M., and R. J. Yinger. 1979. "Teacher Thinking." In *Research on Teaching,* edited by P. L. Peterson and H. J. Walberg, 27–31. Berkeley, CA: McCutchan.

Clifford, G., and J. Guthrie. 1988. *Ed School.* Chicago: University of Chicago Press.

Cobb, P. 1994. "Where Is the Mind? Constructivist and Sociocultural Perspectives on Mathematical Development." *Educational Researcher* 23(7): 13–20.

Cobb, P., and J. Bowers. 1999. "Cognitive and Situated Learning Perspectives in Theory and Practice." *Educational Researcher* 28(2): 4–15.

Cochran-Smith, M., and S. Lytle. 1993. *Inside/Outside: Teacher Research and Knowledge*. New York: Teachers College Press.

———. 1999. "Relationships of Knowledge and Practice: Teacher Learning in Communities." *Review of Research in Education* 24: 249–305.

Cochran-Smith, M., and K. Zeichner, eds. 2005. *Studying Teacher Education: The Report of the AERA Panel on Research and Teacher Education*. Mahwah, NJ: Lawrence Erlbaum Associates.

Constas, M. 1998. "The Changing Nature of Educational Research and a Critique of Postmodernism." *Educational Researcher* 27(2): 26–33.

Cremin, L., D. Shannon, and M. Townsend. 1954. *The History of Teachers College*. New York: Columbia University Press.

Csikszentmihalyi, M. 1991. *Flow: The Psychology of Optimal Experience*. New York: HarperCollins.

Cuban, L. 1990. "Reforming Again, Again, and Again." *Educational Researcher* 19(1): 3–13.

———. 1993. *How Teachers Taught: Constancy and Change in American Classrooms*. New York: Teachers College Press.

Darling-Hammond, L., ed. 1994. *Professional Development Schools: Schools for Developing a Profession*. New York: Teachers College Press.

———. 1999. *Reshaping Teaching Policy, Preparation, and Practice: Influences of the National Board for Professional Teaching Standards*. New York: AACTE Publications.

———. 2000. *Solving the Dilemmas of Teacher Supply, Demand, and Standards: How We Can Ensure a Competent, Caring and Qualified Teacher for Every Child*. New York: National Commission on Teaching and America's Future.

Darling-Hammond, L., A. Wise, and S. Klein. 1995. *A License to Teach: Building a Profession for Twenty-First Century Schools*. Boulder, CO: Westview Press.

de Beauvoir, S. 1952. *The Second Sex*. New York: Knopf.

de Certeau, M. 1984. *The Practices of Everyday Life*. Berkeley: University of California Press.

Dean, M. 1994. *Critical and Effective Histories: Foucault's Methods and Historical Sociology*. New York: Routledge.

Delpit, L. 1995. *Other People's Children: Cultural Conflict in the Classroom*. New York: The New Press.

Derrida, J. 1971. "Structure, Sign, and Play in the Discourse of the Human Sciences." In *The Structural Controversy*, edited by R. Macksey and E. Donato. Baltimore, MD: Johns Hopkins University Press.

Descartes, R. 1637/1954. *La Géométrie*. Trans. D. E. Smith and M. L. Lantham. *The Geometry of René Descartes*. New York: Dover Publications.

Dewey, J. 1902. *The Child and the Curriculum.* Chicago: University of Chicago Press.

———. 1904. "The Relation of Theory to Practice in the Education of Teachers." In *The Third Yearbook of the National Society for the Scientific Study of Education,* edited by C. Murry, 313–338. Chicago: University of Chicago Press.

———. 1933. *How We Think: A Restatement of the Relation of Reflective Thinking to the Educative Process.* Chicago: D. C. Heath.

———. 1938. *Experience and Education.* New York: Macmillan.

———. 1956. *The Child and the Curriculum: The School and the Society.* Chicago: Phoenix Books. (Original work published in 1902).

Doyle, W. 2002. "Narrative and Learning to Teach." A presentation given at the annual meeting of the American Educational Research Association, April 1, New Orleans.

Education Data Partnership. 2000. http://www.ed-data.k12.ca.us. (Accessed January 2002).

Elbaz, F. 1981. "The Teacher's 'Practical Knowledge': Report of a Case Study." *Curriculum Inquiry* 11(1): 43–71.

Elmore, R., P. Peterson, and S. McCarthey. 1996. *Restructuring in the Classroom: Teaching, Learning, and School Organization.* San Francisco, CA: Jossey-Bass.

Emerson, R. W. 2000. *The Essential Writings of Ralph Waldo Emerson.* Edited by B. Atkinson. Princeton, NJ: Princeton Review.

Erickson, E. 1980/1959. *Identity and the Life Cycle.* New York: W. W. Norton.

Erickson, F. 1986. "Qualitative Methods in Teaching." In *Handbook of Research on Teaching,* edited by M. C. Wittrock, 119–161. New York: Macmillan.

Fairclough, N. 1989. *Language and Power.* London: Longman.

Feiman-Nemser, S. 1990. "Teacher Education: Structural and Conceptual Alternatives." In *Handbook of Research on Teacher Education,* edited by W. R. Houston, 212–233. New York: Macmillan.

Feiman-Nemser, S., and M. Buchmann. 1985. "Pitfalls of Experience in Teacher Preparation." *Teachers College Record* 87(1): 53–65.

———. 1986. "Transition to Pedagogical Thinking?" *Journal of Curriculum Studies* 18(3): 239–257.

Festinger, L. 1957. *A Theory of Cognitive Dissonance.* Stanford, CA: Stanford University Press.

Fish, S. 1986. *Is There a Text in This Class? The Authority of Interpretive Communities.* Cambridge, MA: Harvard University Press.

Fiske, J. 1992. "Cultural Studies and the Culture of Everyday Life." In *Cultural Studies,* edited by L. Grossberg et al., 154–173. New York: Routledge.

Florio-Ruane, S. 2002. "More Light: An Argument for Complexity in Studies of Teaching and Teacher Education." *Journal of Teacher Education* 53(3): 203–215.

Fosnot, C., ed. 1996. *Constructivism*. New York: Teachers College Press.

Foster, M. 1998. *Black Teachers on Teaching*. New York: The New Press.

Foucault, M. 1970. *The Order of Things*. Trans. A. M. Sheridan Smith. New York: Vintage Books.

———. 1972. *The Archaeology of Knowledge*. Trans. A. M. Sheridan Smith. London: Tavistock.

———. 1977. *Discipline and Punish*. Trans. C. Gordin et al. New York: Vintage Books.

Freud, S. 1961/1909. *Five Lectures on Psycho-Analysis*. New York: Norton.

Freire, P. 1970. *Pedagogy of the Oppressed*. Trans. M. B. Ramos. New York: Continuum.

———. 1987. *Literacy: Reading the Word and the World*. Trans. D. Macedo. New York: Bergin and Garvey.

Friedan, B. 1963. *The Feminine Mystique*. New York: Norton.

Fullan, M. 1991. *The New Meaning of Educational Change*. New York: Teachers College Press.

Fuller, F., and O. Bown. 1975. "Becoming a Teacher." In *Teacher Education* (74th Yearbook of the National Society for the Study of Education), edited by K. Ryan, Part II, 25–52. Chicago: University of Chicago Press.

Gaardner, J. 1996. *Sophie's World*. New York: Berkley Books.

Galindo, R. 1996. "Reframing the Past in the Present: Chicana Teacher Role Identity as a Bridging Identity." *Education and Urban Society* 29: 85–102.

Gamader, H. 1985. *Philosophical Apprenticeships*. Trans. R. R. Sullivan. Cambridge: MIT Press.

Gardner, H. 1985. *The Mind's New Science: A History of the Cognitive Revolution*. New York: Basic Books.

———. 1991. *The Unschooled Mind*. New York: Basic Books.

———. 1993. *Creating Minds*. New York: Basic Books.

Gee, J. 1992. *The Social Mind: Language, Ideology and Social Practice*. New York: Bergin and Garvey.

———. 1999. *An Introduction to Discourse Analysis*. New York: Routledge.

Geertz, C. 1973. *The Interpretation of Cultures*. New York: Basic Books.

Gerald, D., and W. Hussar. 1998. *Projections of Education Statistics to 2008*. Paper No. NCES 98-016. Washington, DC: National Center for Education Statistics. http://nces.ed.gov. (Accessed January 2002).

Giddens, A. 1979. *Central Problems in Social Theory: Action, Structure, and Contradiction in Social Analysis*. Berkeley: University of California Press.

Gilligan, C. 1982. *In a Different Voice*. Cambridge, MA: Harvard University Press.

Giroux, H. 1992. *Border Crossings: Cultural Workers and the Politics of Education*. New York: Routledge.

Glickman, C., ed. 2004. *Letters to the Next President: What We Can Do About the Real Crisis in Public Education*. New York: Teachers College Press.

Goffman, E. 1959. *The Presentation of Self in Everyday Life.* Garden City, NJ: Doubleday.

———. 1981. *Forms of Talk.* Philadelphia: University of Pennsylvania Press.

Goleman, D. 1996. *Emotional Intelligence: Why It Can Matter More Than IQ.* New York: Bantam Books.

Good, T. L., B. J. Biddle, and J. E. Brophy. 1978. *Teachers Make a Difference.* New York: Holt, Rinehart and Winston.

Gore, J. 1998. "Disciplining Bodies: On the Continuity of Power Relations in Pedagogy." In *Foucault's Challenge: Discourse, Knowledge, and Power in Education,* edited by T. Popkewitz and M. Brennan, 231–254. New York: Teachers College Press.

Grant, C., and C. Sleeter. 2006. *Turning on Learning: Five Approaches for Multicultural Teaching Plans for Race, Class, Gender and Disability.* Hoboken, NJ: Wiley.

Gray, J. 1993. *Men Are from Mars, Women Are from Venus.* New York: Harper-Collins.

Greene, B. 1999. *The Elegant Universe: Superstrings, Hidden Dimensions, and the Quest for the Ultimate Theory.* New York: Vantage.

Greeno, J. 1997. "On Claims That Answer the Wrong Questions." *Educational Researcher* 26(1): 5–17.

Grice, H. P. 1968. "Utterer's Meaning, Sentence-Meaning, and Word-Meaning." *Foundations of Language* 4: 1–18.

———. 1975. "Logic and Conversation." In *Syntax and Semantics 3: Speech Acts,* edited by P. Cole and J. Morgan, 41–48. New York: Academic Press.

Grondin, J. 1994. *Introduction to Philosophical Hermeneutics.* New Haven, CT: Yale University Press.

Grossman, P. 1990. *The Making of a Teacher: Teacher Knowledge and Teacher Education.* New York: Teachers College Press.

Grossman, P. L., S. M. Wilson, and L. Shulman. 1989. "Teachers of Substance: Subject Matter Knowledge for Teaching." In *Knowledge Base for the Beginning Teacher,* edited by M. C. Reynolds, 23–36. Oxford: Pergamon Press.

Gruber, H., and J. Voneche, eds. 1977. *The Essential Piaget.* New York: Basic Books.

Gudmundsdottir, S., and L. Shulman. 1987. "Pedagogical Content Knowledge in Social Studies." *Scandinavian Journal of Educational Research* 31: 59–70.

Gudykunst, W., S. Tong-Toomey, and T. Nishida, eds. 1996. *Communication in Personal Relationships Across Cultures.* Thousand Oaks, CA: Sage Publications.

Gumperz, J. 1982. *Discourse Strategies.* Cambridge: Cambridge University Press.

Haberman, M. 1990. "Urban Teachers Who Quit: Why They Leave and What They Do." *Urban Education* 25(3): 297–303.

————. 1994. "Gentle Teaching in a Violent Society." *Educational Horizons* 72(30): 131–135.

————. 1995. *Star Teachers of Children in Poverty.* West Lafayette, IN: Kappa Delta Pi.

————. n.d. "Star Teacher On-Line Screener." The Haberman Educational Foundation. http://www.altcert.org/teacher/the_test.asp. (Accessed July 2007).

Habermas, J. 1984. *Theory of Communicative Action,* Vol. 1: *Reason and the Rationalization of Society.* Trans. T. McCarthy. London: Heinemann.

Hamachek, D. 1999. "Effective Teachers: What They Do, How They Do It, and the Importance of Self-Knowledge." In *The Role of Self in Teacher Development,* edited by R. Lipka and T. Brinthaupt, 189–224. Albany: State University of New York Press.

Hanushek, E. A., J. F. Kain, and S. G. Rivkin. 2004. "The Revolving Door." *Education Next* 4(1): 76–82.

Hargreaves, A. 1995. *Changing Teachers, Changing Times: Teachers' Work and Culture in the Postmodern Age.* London: Cassell.

Heidegger, M. 1997/1927. *Being and Time: A Translation of* Sein und Zeit. Trans. J. Stambaugh. Albany: State University of New York Press.

Helms, J. 1990. "Toward a Model of White Racial Identity Development." In *Black and White Racial Identity: Theory, Research, and Practice,* edited by J. Helms, 49–80. New York: Greenwood.

Henke, R., X. Chen, and S. Geis. 2000. "Progress Through the Teacher Pipeline: 1992–1993 College Graduates and Elementary/Secondary School Teaching as of 1997." Paper No. NCES 2000152. Washington, DC: National Center for Education Statistics.

Herbst, J. 1991. *And Sadly Teach.* Madison: University of Wisconsin Press.

Herrnstein, R., and C. Murray. 1996. *The Bell Curve: Intelligence and Class Structure in American Life.* New York: Free Press.

Hess, F. 2001. *Tear Down This Wall: The Case for a Radical Overhaul of Teacher Certification.* Washington, DC: Progressive Policy Institute.

Hirsch, E. D., Jr. 1987. *Cultural Literacy: What Every American Needs to Know.* New York: Vintage Books.

Hoffman-Kipp, P., and B. Olsen. 2007. "Accessing Praxis: Practicing Theory, Theorizing Practice in Social Justice Teachers' First Year of Teaching." In *Teacher Education with an Attitude,* edited by M. Finn and P. Finn. Albany: State University of New York Press.

Holland, D., W. Lachiocotte, D. Skinner, and C. Cain. 1998. *Identity and Agency in Cultural Worlds.* Cambridge, MA: Harvard University Press.

Holquist, M. 1990. *Dialogism: Bakhtin and His World.* London: Routledge.

Holt-Reynolds, D. 1992. "Personal History–Based Beliefs as Relevant Prior Knowledge in Course Work." *American Educational Research Journal* 29(2): 325–349.

hooks, b. 1993. *Teaching to Transgress*. New York: Routledge.

Hunter, M. 1982. *Mastery Teaching: Increasing Instructional Effectiveness in Secondary Schools, Colleges, and Universities*. El Segundo, CA: TIP.

Hussar, W., and T. Bailey. 2006. "Projections of Education Statistics to 2015." Paper No. NCES 2006-084. U.S. Department of Education, National Center for Education Statistics. Washington, DC: U.S. Government Printing Office.

Hymes, D. 1972. "Introduction" to C. Cazden's *The Functions of Language in the Classroom*, xi–lvii. New York: Teachers College Press.

Ingersoll, R. 2003. *Who Controls Teachers' Work: Power and Accountability in America's Schools*. Cambridge, MA: Harvard University Press.

———. 2004. "Why Do High-Poverty Schools Have Difficulty Staffing Their Classrooms with Qualified Teachers?" A report prepared for Renewing Our Schools, Securing Our Future: A National Task Force on Public Education. Washington, DC: Center for American Progress.

Jackson, P. 1986. *The Practice of Teaching*. New York: Teachers College Press.

Jameson, F. 1991. *Postmodernism, or, the Cultural Logic of Late Capitalism*. Durham, NC: Duke University Press.

Jones, F. 1987. *Positive Classroom Discipline* (Video Series). New York: McGraw-Hill.

Jung, C. G. 1970. *Psychiatric Studies*, 2nd ed. Princeton, NJ: Princeton University Press.

Kagan, D. 1992. "Implications of Research on Teacher Belief." *Educational Psychologist* 27(1): 65–90.

Kant, I. 1781/2003. *Critique of Pure Reason*. New York: Dover Publications.

Kaptchuck, T. 1983. *Chinese Medicine: The Web That Has No Weaver*. London: Random House.

Kelchtermans, G. 1996. "Teacher Vulnerability: Understanding Its Moral and Political Roots." *Cambridge Journal of Education* 26(3): 307–323.

Kelly, G. 1955. *The Psychology of Personal Constructs*. New York: W. W. Norton.

———. 1963. *A Theory of Personality*. New York: W. W. Norton.

Kim, E., and R. Kellough. 1998. "Establishing and Maintaining an Effective and Safe Classroom Learning Environment." In *A Resource Guide for Secondary School Teaching*. Englewood Cliffs, NJ: Prentice Hall.

King, J. 2004. "Paige Calls NEA 'Terrorist Organization.'" *CNN News Post*, Monday, February 23. www.cnn.com/2004/EDUCATION/02/23/paige.terrorist.nea.

Kirshner, D., and J. Whitson. 1998. "Obstacles to Understanding Cognition as Situated." *Educational Researcher* 27(8): 22–28.

Kliebard, H. 1995. *The Struggle for the American Curriculum*. New York: Routledge.

Knapp, T. 1999. "Response to Elliot W. Eisner's 'The Promise and Perils of Alternative Forms of Data Representation.'" *Educational Researcher* 28(1): 18–19.

Knowles, J. G. 1992. "Models for Understanding Pre-Service and Beginning Teachers' Biographies: Illustrations from Case Studies." In *Studying Teachers' Lives*, edited by I. Goodson, 99–152. New York: Teachers College Press.

Kohl, H. R. 1991. *I Won't Learn from You: The Role of Assent in Learning*. Minneapolis, MN: Milkweed Editions.

Kornfield, J. 1993. *A Path with Heart*. New York: Bantam.

Korthagen, F., and J. Kessels. 1999. "Linking Theory and Practice: Changing the Pedagogy of Teacher Education." *Educational Researcher* 28(4): 4–17.

Kozol, J. 1991. *Savage Inequalities: Children in America's Schools*. New York: HarperPerennial.

Krashen, S. 1987. *Principles and Practice in Second Language Acquisition*. Boston: Prentice-Hall International.

Kuhn, T. 1977. *The Structure of Scientific Revolutions*. Chicago: The University of Chicago Press.

Lagemann, E. 2000. *An Elusive Science: The Troubling History of Education Research*. Chicago: The University of Chicago Press.

Lakoff, G., and M. Johnson. 1980. *Metaphors We Live By*. Chicago: The University of Chicago Press.

Lakoff, G., and M. Turner. 1989. *More Than Cool Reason: A Field Guide to Poetic Metaphor*. Chicago: The University of Chicago Press.

Lakoff, R. 1973. "The Logic of Politeness: Or, Minding Your P's and Q's." *CLS, Proceedings of the Chicago Linguistics Society*, 292–305.

———. 1990. *Talking Power: The Politics of Language*. New York: Basic Books.

Lampert, M., and D. Ball. 1998. *Teaching, Multimedia, and Mathematics: Investigations of Real Practice*. New York: Teachers College Press.

Lanier, J., and J. W. Little. 1986. "Research on Teacher Education." In *Handbook of Research on Teaching*, 3rd ed., edited by M. C. Wittrock, 527–569. New York: Macmillan.

Lankford, H., S. Loeb, and J. Wyckoff. 2002. "Teacher Sorting and the Plight of Urban Schools: A Descriptive Analysis." *Educational Evaluation and Policy Analysis* 24(1): 37–62.

Lave, J. 1988. *Cognition in Practice: Mind, Mathematics, and Culture in Everyday Life*. Cambridge: Cambridge University Press.

Lave, J., and E. Wenger. 1991. *Situated Learning*. Cambridge: Cambridge University Press.

Leinhardt, G., and J. Greeno. 1986. "The Cognitive Skill of Teaching." *Journal of Educational Psychology* 78(2): 75–95.

Leinhardt, G., and D. Smith. 1985. "Expertise in Mathematics Instruction: Subject Matter Knowledge." *Journal of Educational Psychology* 77(3): 247–271.

Lemann, N. 1999. *The Big Test: The Secret History of the American Meritocracy*. New York: Farrar, Straus and Giroux.

Lemert, C. 1997. *Postmodernism Is Not What You Think*. London: Blackwell.

Leo, J. 2002. "Carping in Harvard Yard." *U.S. News & World Report,* January 21: 53.

Levin, B., and P. Ammon. 1992. "The Development of Beginning Teachers' Pedagogical Thinking: A Longitudinal Analysis of Four Case Studies." *Teacher Education Quarterly* 19(4): 19–37.

Lewin, K. 1948. *Resolving Social Conflicts.* New York: Harper and Row.

Lieberman, A. 1995. "Practices That Support Teacher Development." *Phi Delta Kappan* 76(8): 591–596.

Linde, C. 1993. *Life Stories: The Creation of Coherence.* New York: Oxford University Press.

Little, J. W. 1990. "The Persistence of Privacy: Autonomy and Initiative in Teachers' Professional Relations." *Teachers College Record* 91(4): 509–536.

Lloyd, M., and A. Thacker, eds. 1997. *The Impact of Michel Foucault on the Social Sciences and Humanities.* London: Macmillan.

Lortie, D. 1975. *Schoolteacher: A Sociological Study.* Chicago: University of Chicago Press.

Luke, A. 1995. "Text and Discourse in Education: An Introduction to Critical Discourse Analysis." In *Review of Research in Education* 21, edited by M. Apple, 3–48. Washington, DC: AERA.

Lyotard, F. 1984/1979. *The Postmodern Condition.* Minneapolis: University of Minnesota Press.

Martinez, V. 1998. *Parrot in the Oven: My Vida: A Novel.* New York: HarperCollins.

McDaniel, T. 1986. "A Primer on Classroom Discipline: Old and New." *Phi Delta Kappan,* September: 63–67.

McDermott, K. 2007. "'Expanding the Moral Community' or 'Blaming the Victim'? The Politics of State Education Accountability Policy." *American Educational Research Journal* 44(1): 77–111.

McGuinn, P. 2006. *No Child Left Behind and the Transformation of Federal Education Policy, 1965–2006.* Lawrence: University Press of Kansas.

McIntosh, Peggy. 1988. "White Privilege and Male Privilege: A Personal Account of Coming to See Correspondences Through Work in Women's Studies." Working paper. Wellesley, MA: Wellesley College Center for Research on Women.

Mead, G. H. 1964/1932. *Mind, Self, & Society from the Standpoint of a Social Behaviorist.* Chicago: University of Chicago Press.

Mehan, H. 1979. *Learning Lessons: Social Organization in the Classroom.* Cambridge, MA: Harvard University Press.

Meier, D. 1995. *The Power of Their Ideas: Lessons from a Small School in Harlem.* Boston: Beacon Press.

Meier, D., and G. Wood, eds. 2004. *Many Children Left Behind.* Boston: Beacon Press.

Meyer, R. 2000. "What Is the Place of Science in Educational Research?" *Educational Researcher* 29(6): 38–39.

Mezirow, J. 1991. *Transformative Dimensions of Adult Learning.* San Francisco, CA: Jossey-Bass.

Mezirow, J., and Associates. 2000. *Learning as Transformation.* San Francisco, CA: Jossey-Bass.

Miles, M., and M. Huberman. 1984. *Qualitative Data Analysis: A Sourcebook of New Methods.* Beverly Hills, CA: Sage Publications.

Milner, J., and L. Milner. 1998. *Bridging English.* Boston, MA: Prentice Hall.

Mishler, E. 1986. *Research Interviewing: Context and Narrative.* Cambridge: Harvard University Press.

Moffett, J. 1992. *Harmonic Learning.* Portsmouth, NH: Heinemann.

———. 1994. *The Universal Schoolhouse: Spiritual Awakening Through Education.* San Francisco, CA: Jossey-Bass.

Murname, R., J. Singer, J. Wilett, J. Kemple, and R. Olsen. 1991. *Who Will Teach? Policies That Matter.* Cambridge, MA: Harvard University Press.

National Center for Education Statistics (NCES). n.d. *America's Teachers: Profile of a Profession.* Washington, DC: Office of Educational Research and Improvement.

National Commission on Teaching and America's Future (NCTAF). 1996. *What Matters Most: Teaching for America's Future.* New York: National Commission on Teaching and America's Future.

———. 2003. "No Dream Denied: A Pledge to America's Children." http://www.nctaf.org. (Accessed March 2, 2004).

National Education Association. 1993. "Report of the Committee of Secondary School Studies." Washington, DC: U.S. Government Printing Office.

Natoli, J., and L. Hutcheon, eds. 1993. *A Postmodern Reader.* Albany: State University of New York Press.

Oakes, J., and M. Lipton. 2003. *Teaching to Change the World,* 3rd ed. Boston: McGraw Hill.

Ogbu, J. 1988. "Literacy and Schooling in Subordinate Cultures." In *Perspectives on Literacy,* edited by E. Kintgen, B. Kroll, and M. Rose, 227–242. Carbondale: Southern Illinois University Press.

———. 1990a. "Minority Education in Comparative Perspective." *The Journal of Negro Education* (59)1: 45–57.

Ogbu, J., with H. D. Simons. 1990b. "Voluntary and Involuntary Minorities: A Cultural-Ecological Theory of School Performance with Some Implications for Education." *Anthropology and Education Quarterly* 29(2): 155–188.

Olsen, B., and L. Anderson. 2007. "Courses of Action: A Qualitative Investigation into Urban Teacher Retention and Career Development." *Urban Review* 42(1): 5–29.

Olsen, B., and L. Kirtman. 2002. "Teacher as Mediator of School Reform: An Examination of Teacher Practice in 36 California Restructuring Schools." *Teachers College Record* 104(2): 301–324.

Pajares, M. 1992. "Teachers' Beliefs and Educational Research: Cleaning Up a Messy Construct." *Review of Educational Research* 62: 307–332.

Piaget, J. 1954. *The Construction of Reality in the Child*. New York: Basic Books.

———. 1972. "Intellectual Development from Adolescence to Adulthood." *Human Development* 15: 1–12.

Popkewitz, T. 2001. "Dewey, Vygotsky, and the Social Administration of the Individual: Constructivist Pedagogy as Systems of Ideas in Historical Spaces." *American Educational Research Journal* 35(4): 535–570.

Popkewitz, T., and M. Brennan, eds. 1998. *Foucault's Challenge: Discourse, Knowledge, and Power in Education*. New York: Teachers College Press.

Powell, R., J. McLaughlin, T. Savage, and S. Zehm. 2001. *Classroom Management: Perspectives on the Social Curriculum*. Upper Saddle River, NJ: Merrill Prentice Hall.

Putnam, R., and H. Borko. 2000. "What Do New Views of Knowledge and Thinking Have to Say About Research on Teacher Learning?" *Educational Researcher* 29(1): 4–16.

Quinn, N., and D. C. Holland, eds. 1987. *Cultural Models in Language and Thought*. New York: Cambridge University Press.

Quiocho, A., and F. Rios. 2000. "The Power of Their Presence: Minority Group Teachers and Schooling." *Review of Educational Research* 70(4): 485–528.

Ravitch, D. 2000. *Left Back: A Century of Battles over School Reform*. New York: Touchstone Books.

Rosaldo, R. 1989. *Culture and Truth: The Remaking of Social Analysis*. Boston, MA: Beacon Press.

Rust, F. 1994. "The First Year of Teaching: It's Not What They Expected." *Teaching and Teacher Education* 10(2): 205–217.

Sacks, H., E. Schegloff, and G. Jefferson. 1974. "A Simplest Systematics of the Organization of Turn-Taking in Conversation." *Language* 50: 696–735.

Sagan, C. 1993. *Cosmos*. New York: Ballantine Books.

Sarason, S. 1981. *The Culture of the School and the Problem of Change*. Boston, MA: Allyn and Bacon.

Scheibe, K. E. 1995. *Self Studies: The Psychology of Self and Identity*. Westport, CT: Praeger.

Schiefele, U. 1991. "Interest, Learning and Motivation." *Educational Psychiatrist* 26(3 and 4): 299–323.

Schiefele, U., and M. Csikszentmihalyi. 1993. "Interest and the Quality of Experience in Classrooms." Paper prepared for the *European Journal of Psychology of Education*, Munich.

Schiffrin, D. 1994. *Approaches to Discourse*. Oxford: Blackwell.

Schön, D. 1987. *Educating the Reflective Practitioner.* San Francisco, CA: Jossey-Bass.

Scollon, R., and S. W. Scollon. 2001. "Intercultural Communication: A Discourse Approach." *Language in Society* 21. Oxford, UK: Blackwell.

Shavelson, R. J., and P. Stern. 1981. "Research on Teachers' Pedagogical Thoughts, Judgments, Decisions and Behaviors." *Review of Education Research* 51: 455–498.

Shulman, L. 1986a. "Those Who Understand: Knowledge Growth in Teaching." *Educational Researcher* 15(2): 4–14.

———. 1986b. "Paradigms and Research Programs in the Study of Teaching: A Contemporary Perspective." In *Handbook of Research on Teaching,* 3rd ed., edited by M. C. Wittrock, 3–36. New York: Macmillan.

———. 1987. "Knowledge and Teaching: Foundations of the New Reform." *Harvard Educational Review* 57(1): 1–22.

Singer, J. 1972. *Boundaries of the Soul: The Practice of Jung's Psychology.* New York: Doubleday.

Sisken, L. 1994. *Realms of Knowledge: Academic Departments in Secondary Schools.* London: Falmer Press.

Sprinthall, N., A. Reiman, and L. Thies-Sprinthall. 1996. "Teacher Professional Development." In *Handbook of Research on Teacher Education,* edited by J. Sikula, 666–703. New York: Macmillan.

St. John Hunter, C., and D. Harman. 1979. *Adult Illiteracy in the United States.* New York: McGraw-Hill.

Steinberg, J. 1998. "The Changing Face of America's Teachers." *New York Times Magazine,* April 5: 26–32.

Stenhouse, L. 1975. *An Introduction to Curriculum Research and Development.* London: Heinemann.

Street, B. 1984. *Literacy in Theory and Practice.* Cambridge: Cambridge University Press.

Street, B., ed. 1993. *Cross-Cultural Approaches to Literacy.* Cambridge: Cambridge University Press.

Sykes, G. 1999. "Introduction: Teaching as Learning Profession." In *Teaching as the Learning Profession,* edited by L. Darling-Hammond and G. Sykes, xv–xxi. San Francisco, CA: Jossey-Bass.

Tannen, D. 1993. "What's in a Frame?" In *Framing in Discourse,* edited by D. Tannen, 14–54. New York: Oxford University Press.

Tatum, B. 1999. *Why Are All the Black Kids Sitting Together in the Cafeteria? And Other Conversations About Race.* New York: Basic Books.

Taylor, C. 1985. *Human Agency and Language: The Philosophical Papers 1.* Cambridge: Cambridge University Press.

Thoreau, H. D. 1854. *Walden.* Boston: J. R. Osgood.

Tremmel, R. 1993. "Zen and the Art of Reflective Practice in Teacher Education." *Harvard Educational Review* 63(4): 434–458.

Tyack, D., and L. Cuban. 1995. *Tinkering Toward Utopia: A Century of Public School Reform.* New York: Teachers College Press.

U.S. Department of Education. 2002. *Meeting the Highly Qualified Teachers Challenge: The Secretary's Annual Report on Teacher Quality.* Washington, DC: Author.

———. n.d. *No Child Left Behind Information Centers.* www.ed.gov/nclb. (Accessed July 2007).

Valli, L. 1995. "The Dilemma of Race: Learning to Be Colorblind and Color Conscious." *Journal of Teacher Education* 46(2): 120–129.

Veenman, S. 1984. "Perceived Problems of Beginning Teachers." *Review of Educational Research* 54(2): 143–178.

Vygotsky, L. 1978. *Mind in Society.* Cambridge, MA: Harvard University Press.

Waddington, C. 1956. *Principles of Embryology.* London: George Allen and Unwin Ltd.

Weinstein, C. 1989. "Teacher Education Students' Preconceptions of Teaching." *Journal of Teacher Education* (March–April): 53–60.

———. 1990. "Prospective Elementary Teachers' Beliefs About Teaching: Implications for Teacher Education." *Teaching and Teacher Education* 6(3): 279–299.

West, C. 1993. *Race Matters.* Boston: Beacon Press.

Wexler, E., L. Carlos, and J. A. Izu. 1998. *California's Class Size Reduction: Implications for Equity, Practice, and Implementation.* San Francisco, CA: PACE/WestEd.

Wideen, M., J. Mayer-Smith, and B. Moon. 1998. "A Critical Analysis of the Research on Learning to Teach: Making the Case for an Ecological Perspective on Inquiry." *Review of Educational Research* 68(2): 130–178.

Will, G. 2006. "Ed Schools Versus Education: Prospective Teachers Are Expected to Have the Correct 'Disposition,' Proof of Which Is Espousing 'Progressive' Political Beliefs." *Newsweek,* January 16.

Willis, P. 1981. *Learning to Labor: How Working Class Kids Get Working Class Jobs.* New York: Columbia University Press.

Wilson, S. M., L. Shulman, and A. Richert. 1987. "'150 Different Ways of Knowing': Representations of Knowledge in Teaching." In *Exploring Teachers' Thinking,* edited by J. Calderhead, 104–124. London: Cassell.

Wineburg, S., and S. Wilson. 1991. "Subject-Matter Knowledge in the Teaching of History." *Advances in Research on Teaching,* Vol. 2, 305–347.

Woods, P. 1996. *Researching the Art of Teaching: Ethnography for Educational Use.* London: Routledge.

Zeichner, K. 1992. "Conceptions of Reflective Teaching in Contemporary United States Teacher Education Program Reforms." In *Reflective Teacher Education: Cases and Critiques,* edited by L. Valli. Albany: State University of New York Press.

———. 1999. "The New Scholarship in Teacher Education." *Education Researcher* 28(9): 4–15.

Zeichner, K., and J. Gore. 1990. "Teacher Socialization." In *Handbook of Research on Teacher Education,* edited by W. R. Houston, 329–348. New York: Macmillan.

Zeichner, K., and D. Liston. 1990. "Traditions of Reform in U.S. Teacher Education." *Journal of Teacher Education* 4(12): 3–20.

Zeichner, K., and B. Tabachnick. 1981. "Are the Effects of Teacher Education Washed Out by School Experience?" *Journal of Teacher Education* 32(3): 7–11.

Zhing-yi, Yuan-zhu, Xuan-du (Beijing Institute of Traditional Chinese Medicine). 1978. *Lao Tzu.* Beijing: People's Press.

Index

About the Author

Brad Olsen is assistant professor of education at the University of California, Santa Cruz. His teaching and research focus on teaching, teachers, and teacher development; critical pedagogy; English education; and sociolinguistics. Before earning his Ph.D. in Education at the University of California, Berkeley, he worked in high schools in Maine, Massachusetts, South America, and California. He earned his A.B. at Bowdoin College and his M.Ed. at the Harvard Graduate School of Education.